RENT STRIKES

PEOPLES' STRUGGLE FOR HOUSING IN WEST SCOTLAND 1890-1916

JOSEPH MELLING

POLYGON BOOKS

First published 1983 by
Polygon Books,
1 Buccleuch Place, Edinburgh, EH8 9LW.

The Publisher wishes to thank George Outram and Co. Ltd. for permission to reproduce photographs from *The Bulletin*, Jonathan Zeitlin for permission to reproduce contemporary pamphlets, and the Mitchell Library for permission to reproduce the cartoon from *The Baillie*.

Typeset in Megaron by
Edinburgh University Student Publications Board.

Designed by Ann Paterson.

Printed by Anchor Press,
Tiptree, Essex.

ISBN 0 904919 72 2

CONTENTS

INTRODUCTION

The industrial, social and political unrest on Clydeside during the First World War has attracted widespread coverage from politicians, intellectuals and writers. Much of the discussion and debate has centred on how 'Red' was the Clyde; did the 1914-18 war constitute a revolutionary opportunity which was missed? From the perspective of political leaders such as Willie Gallacher and John Maclean the answer was emphatically yes.[1] Maclean, drawing confidence from the wartime militancy of the Glasgow working class, declared in 1920:

We can make Glasgow a Petrograd, a revolutionary storm centre second to none.[2]

Recently, some historians have offered a different interpretation of the events on Clydeside; Christopher Harvie declared in 1981:

Forget the Red Clyde; throughout the World War I Scotland was overwhelmingly patriotic.[3]

Although both statements differ in their interpretation of political radicalism on the Clyde, there is general agreement that Clydeside formed the centre of industrial and political strife in Britain at the peak of wartime production. This was manifested in the frequent anti-war demonstrations, home rule agitation, the shop stewards movement, and the Glasgow Rent Strikes. Within this spectrum of activity, historians have focused on different aspects of the Clydeside struggles. James Hinton for example, stressed the role of the engineers and the Clyde Workers' Committee (C.W.C.) in leading the skilled workers' opposition to the introduction of the Munitions Act in June 1915. Other writers, such as Ian Maclean, have focused more closely on the ideological and political views of men such as James Maxton, John Maclean and Tom Bell through an analysis of their activities in separate, political organisations during the First World War.

However, in spite of the wealth of existing studies on Clydeside, comparatively little attention has been directed towards placing the role of working class women in these struggles. In fact, the broader question of identifying the level and nature of women's involvement in the Scottish

Labour Movement during the First World War has remained a neglected area of historical research. A plausible explanation for the lack of focus on women could be attributed to the virtual absence of females employed in shipbuilding and other heavy industries on the Clyde. Nonetheless, this in itself is a crude reflection of the overwhelming attention paid to the workplace as the centre of militancy rather than non-industrial forms of protests which were generated outside it.

Joseph Melling's book provides a notable exception to the rule; from the outset, Melling stresses the equal importance of non-industrial based struggles in shaping working class awareness and organisation. This approach is combined with a lengthy analysis of the mass involvement of working class women in the Rent Strikes of 1915. In adopting this approach, Melling's book represents an important landmark in widening the scope of issues and relationships discussed in the sphere of Labour history.

The book encompasses a wide-range of interesting themes including that of the rise of the Independent Labour Party (I.L.P.) in the west of Scotland and the origins of the party's involvement in the housing issue. It shows how social movements originating in specific localities could ultimately be instrumental in changing Government policy and legislation with respect to the housing question. This theme is exemplified by a lucid portrayal of the way in which the rent strikers in the localities of Govan and Partick succeeded in capturing the support of political parties and industrial organisations. The broader economic, social and political dimensions of the Rent Strikes are skilfully documented and fully referenced in the text. A theme worthy of special attention is Melling's examination of the role of working class women in the Rent Strikes since it provides a welcome opportunity to open up new avenues of inquiry on gender relationships in the Labour movement. Melling's impetus for focusing on women and particularly on housewives, is derived from an appreciation of their crucial role in initiating the Rent Strikes and resisting threats of evictions from landlords.

In accounting for the origins of housewives' discontent, the text draws attention to the growing scarcity in housing provision, increased rents, and the rising cost of living prior to 1915. I shows how the cumulative effects of rising costs had a detrimental effect on the household economy and how it inspired housewives to take direct action of nonpayment of rents as a retaliatory measure against their immediate enemy — landlords. As Melling points out, the feelings of resentment amongst housewives were heightened by their awareness that whilst standards of domestic comfort were extremely low, many of their husbands were sacrificing their lives for their country.

Inspired by a strong sense of injustice, Melling shows how grassroots resistance to the rent increases was organised and conducted; he stresses the importance of long established community enterprises such as the local cooperative society as a regular meeting spot for the local inhabitants. Otherwise, informal gatherings in tenants' homes provided another popular meeting place in which housewives were free to discuss their grievances and tactics over a cup of tea. More official forms of support were provided by the Glasgow and Govan Women's Housing Association in conjunction with the Tenant's Defence Association. Emerging from his account of these Associations is a full appreciation of the key role played by local female campaigners such as Mary Barbour, Helen Crawfurd, Agnes Dollan, and Mary Laird, in providing effective leadership in broadening support for the Rent Strikers on the Clyde. This theme is amplified through an examination of the successful links which were forged between female leaders and industrial workers as expressed through the support of the C.W.C. and the shop stewards movement. The fusion of these elements serves to emphasise the unity and harmony of interests which can exist between the sexes in Labour politics.

Overall, the book raises a number of important issues and questions concerning the level of awareness and involvement of both sexes in the Glasgow Labour movement during the First World War.

Perhaps most importantly, the text highlights the power and capability of working class women to unite and organise a campaign of resistance on their own initiative, outside of the workplace. This was a remarkable feat in view of the subordinate position held by women from all social classes in terms of political and social status. The most obvious manifestation of inequality of opportunity between the sexes was the absence of the vote for women. However a more complex and specific form of oppression was the arduous everyday experience of working class housewives. Many of them encountered acute problems in trying to rear children on a small family budget in order to prevent bad nourishment, ill-health and death. The domestic drudgery which formed the daily experiences of many working class women must inevitably have shaped their own identity in a distinctive way from that of adult male workers, whose jobs revolved around the workplace rather than the confines of the home. This view of women's labour in the home is prevalent in Harry McShane's account of the Scottish Labour Movement:

Most of the socialists were just like other men in their attitudes in the home. Many of them had big families and lived in appalling conditions and it was the women who carried the burden . . . But most of the (socialist) wives were no different from other working class wives — looking after the children and doing hours of housework which was much harder then. They didn't drink, they wouldn't be seen in the pub. They stayed in the home struggling to make ends meet.[4]

Yet in spite of their arduous lives, the housewives of Govan and Partick displayed a strong sense of resilience, allegiance and reaction against their downtrodden circumstances in the hope of improving their lifestyles through cheaper rents, and decent homes. As Melling and others have pointed out, the Rent Strike was identified essentially as a 'women's fight'[5] since it was in tune with their personal experiences and as such, it operated as a springboard for mobilising the mass participation of working class women on the housing issue.

Beyond that, it is difficult to determine the range and diversity of political attitudes amongst the female rank-and-file both during and in the aftermath of the Rent Strikes. Melling's research raises the broader question of the extent to which working class women's involvement on the housing issue was compatible with their broader participation in the women's movement and the Labour movement since both were closely linked with each other in Scotland during this period. This was evident in the representation of both sexes in the I.L.P. Many women were motivated to join the I.L.P. in preference to other political organisations in the knowledge that Keir Hardie, one of the founder members, was a leading advocate of the vote for women. In opening up this area of research it would be interesting to identify the range of attitudes amongst working class housewives on issues such as suffrage, pacifism and politics and to evaluate their links, if any, with other related issues in the women's movement and the Labour movement in Scotland.

From the perspective of female leaders such as Mary Barbour, Helen Crawfurd, and Agnes Dollan, there is strong evidence to suggest that participation in the Rent Strikes formed part of a wider commitment towards the improvement of the political, economic and social status of women in society. Biographical information on the latter two leaders reveal how their personal experiences of sex discrimination fostered much of their later activities in the women's movement and Labour politics.

Agnes Dollan, for example, was forced through family poverty, to leave school, and earn a living at the age of eleven. She found employment in a factory and this was followed by a more regular job as a telephone operator in Glasgow; it was experience of this latter job which inspired Agnes to become a feminist. She was appalled at the long hours which women worked in return for meagre wages and with little promotional prospects. Consequently, she became aware of the need to organise women into a trade union and while still in her teens, she became involved in the Women's Labour League. In addition to her fight for equal employment opportunities, she was committed to the struggle for obtaining political status for women and she joined the Women's Social and Political Union (W.S.P.U.). She fully endorsed the militant tactics adopted by the Pankhursts towards achieving votes for women though does not appear to have been directly involved in any acts of militancy herself.

The outbreak of the First World War represented an intense period of political activity for Agnes Dollan; she was a firm pacifist arguing that:

War is a burden which people cannot afford. Women in particular have no wish for war in which their sons are consumed as fodder.[6]

Alongside her close friend, Helen Crawfurd, a vivacious suffragette and I.L.P.er, she was instrumental in forming the Glasgow branch of the Women's International League, in 1915, and the Women's Peace Crusade in the following year. In terms of her political allegiances, Agnes Dollan was a prominent member of the I.L.P. and was closely allied with her husband Patrick Dollan, in his longstanding ambition to win a Labour majority on Glasgow town council. Thus, it can be seen that female activists such as Agnes Dollan who provided effective leadership in the Rent Strikes, also made an important political contribution in the Scottish Labour movement as a whole.

Drawing from Melling's analysis, it is evident that co-operation between the sexes was a significant ingredient towards ensuring a successful outcome to the Rent Strikes. Undoubtedly, the relationship between female leaders, skilled male workers and Clydeside leaders was to some extent strengthened by their mutual involvement in a close network of political and socialist societies. Political propagandists such as Patrick Dollan, James Maxton, John Maclean and Tom Bell were prominent agitators in the anti-war campaign. Similarly, the I.L.P. and smaller political organisations such as the Socialist Labour Party (S.L.P.) were wholly committed in their support of the housing struggles which in turn formed part of their socialist vision of the provision of good housing for future generations.

It was the fusion of these political and industrial elements, alongside the grassroots support of local housewives and female campaigners which perhaps explains why the Rent Strike was one of the far-reaching achievements of the working class on the Clyde. This victory was exemplified in the passing of the Rent Restriction Act in December 1915.

Melling's book therefore, develops new ways of exploring the level of working class awareness amongst women as expressed through historical events such as the Rent Strikes. It also pinpoints the value of examining the varying forms of interaction between the sexes in a political movement and in doing so serves as a blunt reminder that the Labour movement in Scotland was not entirely the preserve of men.

Helen Corr
Department of Economic History
University of Edinburgh

REFERENCES TO INTRODUCTION

1. W. Gallacher, *Revolt on the Clyde* (1936); and *The Last Memoirs of W. Gallacher* (1966).
2. N. Milton, *John Maclean: In the Rapids of Revolution* (1978). See also P. McKinney, unpublished essay on John Maclean for a discussion of his activities during the First World War (University of Oxford 1982).
3. C. Harvie, 'How Red was the Clyde?' *Scotsman* 18 April 1981 and 'Labour and Scottish Government: The Age of Tom Johnston' in *The Bulletin of Scottish Politics* No. 2 Spring 1981 pp 1-20.
4. H. McShane and J. Smith, *No Mean Fighter* (Pluto Press, 1978), p 34.
5. These were the words of Helen Crawfurd from her personal *Memoirs* located in Marx Memorial Library, London (194?).
6. See H. Corr for biographical information on Helen Crawfurd and Agnes Dollan, forthcoming in W. W. Knox (ed.), *Scottish Labour Leadership 1914-1939: A Biographical Dictionary* (Edinburgh 1983).

Acknowledgements: I would especially like to thank Bill Knox and James Smyth for their useful comments and discussion on this topic.

PREFACE AND ACKNOWLEDGEMENTS

Many people have contributed to my understanding of the rents strikes and working class organisation during the early years of the century. In the original research and explorations I was greatly helped by the reminiscences of the people who allowed me to record their personal accounts of the period and its leading figures. The Barbour family, Harry and William McShane, Ann and Vincent Flynn and those individuals named in the references were always generous with their time and knowledge, whilst the industrial workers and foremen interviewed welcomed my interest in their life and times. Mrs Manchester of Baillies Library placed her encyclopaedic expertise of primary sources at my disposal, and the staff at the Mitchell Library and Glasgow University Library deserve my thanks. The staff of Glasgow University Archives, including Michael Moss, Arnot Wilson and Janet McBain were unusually energetic on my behalf, as were the archivists concerned with the records of the employers' associations I have cited.

Among those who exchanged ideas and sources with me were Sandra Holton, Lou Rosenberg, Alastair Reid and Paul Watchman. I hope that any unpublished material and scholarship has been adequately cited. Earlier drafts of this study have been fairly extensively circulated for reference and comment. Valuable criticism and advice was forthcoming from Geoff Eley, Bert Moorhouse, Alastair Reid and Jerry White, as well as the participants in seminars held at Belfast, Cambridge, Glasgow and London. Ian MacDougall and his colleagues at the Scottish Labour History Society have been supportive and encouraging throughout, and it is upon their work that so much of this study stands. My understanding of the role of women in the struggles was informed by discussions with Helen Corr, Pat Gallagher, Eleanor Gordon, Kathleen Howie, Marie Sproule and Deborah Thom, as well as the projected film study of Christine Bellamy and Jenny Woodley. They have conclusions of their own on these events which may differ from mine. More general, though important, responses came from Keith Burgess, John Foster, Roy Hay, James Hinton, Eric Hobsbawn, Bill Knox, John Saville, Tony Sutcliffe, Steve Tolliday and Jonathan Zeitlin, whilst David Englander often disagreed in a very interesting and informative way. Jason Ditton deserves personal thanks for his invaluable support at a difficult stage in the research and writing, as does Chris Smout for his encouragement of the project. The final revisions of the study were completed at King's College Research Centre, and I should like to thank the fellows and managers of the Centre for their generous assistance. In the production of the book itself, I have been greatly indebted to the Polygon editorial group. In particular I would like to thank Kerry Rankine, Peter Kravitz and Murdo Macdonald for their generous help and advice.

Finally, I would like to think that the story could be read by some of the people whose own families and friends had been engaged in those struggles which sought to change their surroundings in a creative and independent way. It is to them that I'd want to dedicate the study.

Joseph Melling,
January 1983.

CHAPTER ONE

Historical Context: Patrick Geddes to Thomas Jones

In 1919 a strike to secure a working week of 40 hours swept through the great industrial city of Glasgow, led by activists in the engineering trades which had sustained a vital production in the World War of 1914-18. Although the campaign was defeated and the local union leaders disciplined by their national executive, its strength and seriousness further convinced the Government of the dangers posed by the spread of socialist ideas and Labour agitation. When preparing a confidential memorandum for prime minister Lloyd George, a senior Cabinet official outlined some of the main issues which had surfaced since the cessation of military hostilities and the return of the Wartime coalition government to power in the Khaki Election. This official, Thomas Jones, quickly dismissed the suggestion that Bolshevik propaganda and conspiracies were the major force behind the unrest, noting that such beliefs could only take root in 'the soil of genuine grievance', and urged Lloyd George to recognise the expectation of major (and perhaps decisive) changes in the social and industrial conditions encountered by working class people.[1] Turning to the debates on a programme of Social Reconstruction, which had been in evidence since 1917, Jones identified the key questions of hours, wages, housing, land, prices and drink as the substantial areas of reform. Housing was seen as one problem demanding urgent action to relieve present deficiencies and discontents, the memorandum insisting that Lloyd George should press municipal authorities such as Glasgow into immediate commitments, noting that the government should not wait 20 years for a massive rehousing programme but must 'put up in the next five years', hundreds of thousands of homes.[2]

This sense of urgent endeavour was sharpened by the deepening crisis of industrial and social conflict during the the first years of military demobilisation, but also marked a rebirth of the pre-War reforming crusades in which Welsh and Scottish (as well as English) intellectuals had played a leading role. Thomas Jones was himself a late arrival at Whitehall, born at Monmouthshire in 1870 and trained for the Welsh Methodist Chapel before turning to academic studies. Leaving for Glasgow University in 1895, Jones fell under the influence of Sir Henry Jones' moral philosophy as well as the social economics of Christian academics such as the remarkable Professor William Smart and George Adam Smith.[3] Glasgow's intellectual life reached a fresh peak around the turn of the century, as the bitter divisions which had surrounded the Irish Home Rule controversy of 1886 gave way to a new generation of concerns with social conditions and the role of the state in remedying contemporary problems. The strong religious and moral convictions which had guided the followers of Thomas Chalmers and other spiritual leaders in Victorian Scotland remained, as the Glasgow Presbytery conducted its own enquiries into housing conditions or distress amongst the unemployed, but the teachers and students at the University and colleges were anxious to expose social deprivation as the proper subject for scholarly enquiry and civil action. Distanced from the Hegelian discourse of the 1870s and '80s, with its emphasis on positive freedoms through State intervention, men such as George Adam Smith combined a real belief in thrift institutions and savings banks with a doctrine of social responsibility. William Smart built upon the work of public health pioneers such as Dr Russell, delivering his free public lectures on *The Housing Problem and Municipality* to large audiences in 1902, which reiterated the rigorous personal and public obligations of muscular Calvinism whilst acknowledging the duties of municipal authorities in securing fundamental improvements in urban conditions.

It was amidst this ferment of discussion and initiatives that Thomas Jones began his own university and public career, arriving to find the new Gothic buildings crowning Gilmorehill and dominating the west end of Glasgow. Beneath the elegant stone circuses around the civilised River Kelvin and beyond the boundaries of culture marked by the imposing Art Gallery, lay the industrial suburbs of Partick and Whiteinch bordering the great working river of Clydeside. Perched on the promontory which overlooked both privileged and proletarian groups, the ancient university developed a close — if uneasy — relationship with working class tenement districts at this period. Participating in the Students' Settlement campaigns,

Thomas Jones moved on to help found the University Fabian Society and joined the local branch of the Independent Labour Party at nearby Partick. Through the gifted feminist who became his wife, he met such outstanding suffrage leaders as Mary Macarthur, Mrs Bruce Glasier and Mrs Pethick Lawrence. Assistant to Professor Smart from 1901, Jones engaged in a range of progressive causes and municipal issues such as housing debates as well as visiting the great forum of reformist discussion in the London School of Economics before departing Glasgow to serve the Royal Commission on the Poor Laws (and Beatrice Webb) as Special Investigator.[4] At the age of 46 he joined the new cabinet secretariat under Lloyd George in 1916.

Only a year before this, one of the most influential books on the growth of cities and their problems appeared, written with the particular experience of Edinburgh and other Scottish cities in mind. Patrick Geddes presented *Cities in Evolution* as a contribution to a new urban sociology as well as a treatise upon rational town planning and social provision. Like earlier writers such as Matthew Arnold, Geddes was deeply concerned with the cultural consequences of building blight and aesthetic standards found in industrial society. Secure societies could only be developed on the basis of harmonious design and a sensible distribution of space, and even in Edinburgh he detected numerous examples of architectural distortion which he traced to the acquisitive society, noting the long dormitory corridors of tenements in which skilled workmen, 'our foremen and guards, even our clerks' were housed.[5] Instead of revealing a clear ascent towards civilised accommodation for all social classes, the evolution of cities had produced only slums, semi-slums and super-slums for the lower, middle and upper ranks of urban society.[6]

Geddes had fortunately begun to recognise signs of genuine progress in the Garden City movement inaugurated by visionaries such as Howard and Unwin, contributing to what Geddes termed the new or 'neotechnic' city of the future. Praising the 'systematic Utopianism' of the Garden City advocates, Geddes saw a whole new urban order dawning, characterised 'by electricity, hygiene and art, by efficient and beautiful town planning'.[7] The civic exhibitions organised by the Garden Cities Association and others reflected a growing awareness of the distinctive features of an urban society, encouraging the city-dwellers who attended such public displays to participate in municipal politics as a way of securing improved living conditions.[8] The art of urban engineering would be assisted by the extension of social enquiry and by the rebirth of sociology 'as above all the Science of Cities'.[9] Excessive though such passages appear, there is little doubt that the town planning movement and the debates around the great social investigations (including the work of the Webbs and the Royal Commission on the Poor Laws), generated a fresh approach to the question of housing for the broad mass of the population before 1918. Scottish academics, professionals, legal experts and politicians were aware of the comparisons drawn between their cities and industrial districts, and the housing conditions which existed south of the Border. Beautiful monuments and Enlightenment terraces in Edinburgh attracted visiting architects without obscuring the squalid conditions of the poorer districts documented by Geddes, whilst in Glasgow the second imperial city possessed some of the most cancerous slum districts then standing.

Patrick Geddes and Thomas Jones were in many respects the best representatives of a whole generation of intellectuals attempting to influence the Edwardian governments to direct the improvement of British cities, though each only acquired a real reputation after the outbreak of War. More fundamentally, there were a solid series of investigations and enactments before and during the War which transformed the relationship of the State to social problems and ensured greater involvement in meeting the housing needs of working people. Recent research has illustrated the various ways in which ideologies of town planning and garden cities influenced the construction of government industrial housing projects at Woolwich and permeated official thinking on the design and distribution of post-War housing.[10] Yet it would be mistaken to see intellectuals as a coherent social or political force in these years, or the progress of policy-making as the outcome of an interplay between astute civil servants (or their political masters) and the choices offered by the pacifying imagery of the garden city suburb. These groups were unquestionably important actors in the formulation of official and acceptable responses to the changing conditions of social need, but the way in which these needs were discovered and defined did not depend upon their deliberations. Between the 1890s and the outbreak of War there is a discernible shift in the popular attitudes towards such everyday conditions as housing provision, which suggests a more fundamental change in the nature of politics itself during these years. Not only did alliances and priorities change with the growing self-confidence of industrial organisation and the formation of an independent Labour party to represent working people, but inevitable and natural circumstances were increasingly defined as 'problems' capable of political resolution by organised intervention. Such a realisation did not wait upon the findings of a Royal Commission on poverty or industrial housing, but accompanied fresh forms of organisation and debate which involved a new departure in popular participation in politics.

Nor did the struggles and campaigns of the pre-War and Wartime years flow directly from the objective conditions of industrial capitalism or any coherent pattern of housing deficiency and exploitation. The difficulties experienced in the pre-War years were greatly exacerbated by the constraints of Wartime production, but these conditions did not dictate any clear logic of action any more than they followed any predictable pattern of capitalist development. The circumstances in which workplace and urban conflicts were to converge could not be projected from any reading of class relations before the War, though the possibilities for antagonism were evident to even global theorists such as Geddes. By the time both men were to offer their prescriptions on the housing problem, that problem had moved from the realms of an unacceptable blemish on modern society to being one of the central issues in class relations after the War. It was the culmination of the experiences of 1911-1919 that was to prove decisive in the recharting of the housing question, within a wider geography of British State politics.

Many accounts of the Wartime struggles focus upon the dramatic events of 1915-16 in the west of Scotland, which gave birth to the celebrated testaments of 'Red Clydeside' and the subsequent identification of the whole area as a stronghold of socialist sentiment. The older mythology of revolutionary mobilisation has been effectively challenged in recent studies of labour agitations, though the focus has usually remained firmly fixed on the industrial confrontations over such issues as the workplace dilution programme introduced by the Wartime State. More importantly, the encounters between shop stewards and government officials have often been portrayed as a crucial extension of class struggle from the economic to the political sphere, giving birth to a politicised shop floor movement. The relationship between workplace conflict and other forms of organised resistance, or between property-holding and political identities, has been only rarely discussed. Working class politics is generally located as an alternating emphasis between the workplace and the established electoral system, encompassed by a prevailing ideology of 'Labourism' which restricts class expression to the avenues of bourgeois hegemony. Closer examination of campaigns such as the rent strikes of west Scotland during the War, however, suggests that there is a longer and more complex genealogy of non-industrial struggles than existing accounts allow, and that their contribution to the shaping of working class politics is as important as that of work-based organisations. The following narrative outlines the housing conditions facing working class families in Scotland before the War, and the connections between people in different areas of organised struggle at this time. Political dignitaries such as Lloyd George and Thomas Jones figure in the subsequent story of Wartime activities, but their presence should not overshadow the more fundamental achievement of local campaigners in transforming the outlook and loyalties of working people from a liberal world-order to an assertion of labour's independent interest.

CHAPTER TWO

Tenants and the household economy in Clydeside political relations before 1914

Glasgow acquired a reputation for poor housing as early as the 1840s, when the city's wynds were identified as a 'tangle of crime, filth and pestilence' by Frederick Engels.[11] The growing concern at serious epidemics led to an early slum clearance project during the 1860s and '70s, though investigators continued to uncover horrific examples of bulging walls and water-sodden basements in such areas as Cowcaddens until the eve of the First World War itself.[12] Yet the problem had become far more serious than the regular exposés of degraded dwellings by that period: for after 1907, declining profitability and stagnant rent levels had caused the virtual collapse of private construction for working class rental.[13] It was this general crisis in the market relationship between housing demand and building returns that formed the immediate background to the pre-War urban struggles that figure in Scottish newspaper columns *before* the wartime conditions transformed localised problems into a national emergency.

Scotland's heritage of powerful landed interests and building restrictions gave it a peculiar position in the calendar of housing problems at this time. Besides the direct levy of feu rents on the ground, there were at least four distinct factors contributing to this predicament. The most noticeable feature of Scottish cities and towns during the 19th century was probably the preservation of the high-rise tenement block as the typical dwelling. This has been accounted for in explanations ranging from the need for military fortification and French architectural styles, to the simple operation of market force which decreed the maximum usage of land burdened with fixed rents.[14] Whatever the origins of the tenement form, there is little doubt of a strong preference for its continuation by landlords and tenants alike. This cultural support was reinforced by the fairly stringent building regulations implicit in the Dean of Guild approval of lining plans throughout Scotland, and the small-scale organisation of contruction which ensured the continuity of a tenement block within one street. The consequence was an extremely expensive stone structure with an elaborate style of access and layout, accompanied by careful surfacing in the more respectable type of 'close' or entrance.[15] This inevitably increased the costs of construction and led to a situation where, according to Glasgow sanitary inspector Peter Fyfe, 'the labouring class are at present compelled to pay for what is termed "substantiality" in structure . . . in excess of actual requirements.'[16] Less attention was paid to their internal facilities or the basic space required by a growing family, with wash-houses, lavatories and even water supply provided only for a whole tenement or floor.

The second contributory factor appeared in the workings of the property market and its dependence upon capital markets in the second city of the empire. As the local journal of the property owners put it in 1915:[17]

In a general sense the history of any important centre is epitomised in the study of its Property Market. Glasgow, with a population of over a million . . . is a typical example of this. . . . Housing is a first necessity.

Industry needed a large amount of fresh labour, but its provision depended upon available housing or transport and the creation of accommodation was largely beyond the immediate resources of most industrial capitalists. They depended upon other sections of capital investment to generate housing sufficient to sustain the general expansion of regional industry, whilst housebuilders looked particularly to financial institutions and capital markets to raise credit upon which they could complete a sizeable tenement block for sale to purchasers. Speculative building was obviously at its best when a general depression had driven interest rates down and capital was available, whilst labour and materials were likely to be cheaper. Once a general recovery occurred the cost of almost every item increased and incentives were reduced accordingly.

In the Scottish context this variable was rendered more complex and vulnerable by the relative efficiency of the capital markets *and* the widespread practice of mortgage purchasing. The typical owner of tenement property rented to working people was more likely to belong to the lower middle class than any other group, investing perhaps his life savings in bricks and mortar.[18] Purchase was usually assisted by the raising of capital on the security of the property, owners repaying the loan and interest on this 'bond' within a limited period. One Glasgow paper gave the reliable estimate that over 90% of city housing was under bond mortgage, covering perhaps two-thirds of the estimated value in 1915.[19] In this situation, the thousands of small owners (as well as a minority of large property holders) were anxious at every change in interest rates which might eat further into their margin of unearned income. There was also a general trend towards rising interest rates and improved investment opportunities which affected most sections of finance capital and steadily drew funds away from house purchase after 1900. Unfavourable movements in the terms of trade also burdened the building industry with additional costs for imported materials without relieving the increasing flow of investment overseas before the War. This helps to account for the virtual demise of building for working class occupation in these years, and for the resistance offered by landlords to any changes in their status and power.

This aspect of house financing also points to the third main factor shaping tenement administration and living conditions, that of legal restraint and property agency. The pressures to extract the maximum return from such investment and the overpowering presence of landed interests in Scottish political development, are evident in the repressive actions of Glasgow landlords throughout much of the 19th century and before 1914. Under the law of hypothec, Scottish houseowners were able to seize the personal property of tenants who refused (or were simply unable) to pay the agreed rent. Evictions and confiscation of possessions was a common feature of landlord strategies at this period, thousands of families being ejected every year from dwellings they rented.[20] The actual increase of evictions before 1914, especially in years of economic depression, indicated the intensification of conflict as profits were squeezed.

Tenants were able to retaliate in a variety of ways, from a sudden departure (or 'midnight flitting') to the vandalisation of the property itself. Landlords relied upon a traditional system of rent-collecting and tenant surveillance under experienced 'factors', to counteract such tactics. Like the owners themselves, these factors were highly organised in trade and professional associations during the late 19th century, and by local expertise were able to impose a respect for authority and property amongst working class tenants. Their commission had enabled a minority of large factors to build up sizeable empires of property control, stretching across different areas of the city and often merging with actual ownership of tenements for some firms.[21] Their intimate knowledge of specific properties and tenants, as much as the web of interests and legal connections which held their practice together, allowed such individuals a significant degree of autonomy from the multitude of owners who made up their clients. The position of the owner and factor was strengthened by the customary letting arrangements prevailing in 19th century Glasgow and elsewhere, which stipulated quarterly or even annual letting agreements whereby the tenant advanced a large portion of rent as a deposit paid perhaps some months before entering the tenement flat. Only the poorest property was let for a month or less, and most working class families with regular incomes were expected to accept contracts binding them to one house for six or twelve months.[22] Enforcement of legal liabilities on many tenants took the shape of the officer or clerk from the Sheriff's Court, arriving to issue a warrant of ejectment at a tenement close. After 1890 there were growing numbers of working people prepared to contest the case in such local courts, frequently succeeding in delaying the proceedings well beyond the end of the rental agreement and sitting free in retaliation at the landlord's actions.[23] These were often the families of artisans employed in skilled work who rented the better quality flats in Glasgow and the burghs beyond, rather than the less respectable slum dwellers who could offer less public resistance to the factor and his assistants.

The fourth main element in the growth of Glasgow's housing problems was the character and extent of working class demand for accommodation. There were general cyclical movements common to the building industry as a whole, which assumed particular force in west Scotland. The notorious erratic fluctuations generated by speculative activity and the interdependence with other industrial cycles, resulted in the discord between supply and demand which became evident in the rent levels for working class housing. As manufacturing production expanded, capital and labour was attracted from building projects, even when increased employment and earnings stimulated growing demand for industrial housing. Rents responsed only slowly to the shifts in market demand and were often highest after effective demand had subsided, and much lower during a period of rising employment. On Clydeside, an increasing dependence of the regional economy upon shipbuilding and related trades after 1870 exaggerated this friction between trades as two unusually sensitive and unpredictable industries dominated the housing market.[24] The sustained growth of the shipyards before 1914 disguised the violent oscillations in output and the sharp unevenness between burghs in the pace of house construction. Rapid increases in launchings after 1906 occurred at a time of severe depression throughout the building industry, as boom towns such as Clydebank and Dalmuir imported over 16,000 workers every day and were compelled to rely upon non-market incentives to extend their housing stock.[25]

There was not only short-term uncertainty for those employed in shipbuilding trades as such, but a complex relationship with the construction workforce. Depression in building brought a host of workmen flowing into the woodworking occupations or finishing trades of the shipyards, thereby dampening wage levels for the shipbuilders. Construction was such a massive employer, and many of its stone-working skills so specific to building, that other industries could not absorb the levels of unemployment and casualisation seen after 1900, hence the general depression in real wages, earnings and housing demand.[26] Shipbuilding employers continued to complain of serious shortages of ironworkers or 'black squads' before the War, but very rarely experienced difficulties in attracting woodworkers and painters. Such workmen would travel from all over Clydeside to those yards or engine shops able to offer them employment in the difficult years of Scottish building.

There were equally serious trend factors in the decline of working class housing demand, including the lower levels of real wages common to Scotland during the 19th and 20th centuries.[27] The very features which originally attracted iron-shipbuilding firms to Scotland, lower wages and flexibility of work regulation, also ensured a lower level of earnings and demand. When the real income of working people failed to grow appreciably after the building boom of the 1890s, there was a relatively greater incapacity to demand better housing in the Scottish context. Even where the shortage of housing and rising rents offered a genuine incentive to builders (as at Greenock, Clydebank or Govan), contrary influences in the shape of better investment opportunities and rising costs discouraged speculative commitment. House building for working class families had all but ceased on the eve of the War.

Partick and Govan from genesis to community

The local implications of these general patterns of urban development in west Scotland can be clearly seen in the parallel growth of two key shipbuilding burghs, namely, Partick and Govan. The building of Partick occurred later than its neighbour on the opposite side of the Clyde, and proceeded more quickly, though its tenements were catering for professional and independent people as well as the skilled manual workers who could be seen flocking down to Dumbarton Road at 7 a.m., to enter nearby yards or board ferry and tramways for work in other districts. Partick therefore presented its own contrasts to the thousands of migrants who poured into this booming west end burgh after 1860. Whilst the northern end of the Police Commission area had been carefully planned around elegant circuses on the crown of the raised land of Partickhill, providing desirable residences for the new mercantile and industrial bourgeoisie of prospering Glasgow, the southern end of its province was assembled in more haphazard fashion with less substantial builders racing to complete a handful of tenements before selling these to raise fresh working capital. During the last great building period of 1890-1906, Partick was virtually completed, with 1,600 dwellings provided in the peak year of 1901-02 and ten times that number recorded as the burgh's housing total a decade later. At the same time, Partick had become the most densely populated local authority in Scotland by holding 66 people per acre of its land.[28] Like Govan, it had a remarkably large number of people congregated within a substantial but crowded area of land which fronted on to the river and was an important focal point for the traffic of goods and people around a main 'Cross' or crossroads.

The ownership of tenements in both areas seems to have been a fragmented and complicated affair, with a confusing variety of investors and interests involved in housing transactions. One important local study of Partick indicates that local employers (including shipfurnishing, railway and subway owners) were amongst the most substantial of owners, but that they held only a few tenements each, whilst the local authorities and Partick Co-operative Society also housed their employees in employers' housing. Legal and professional groups were prominent in the purchase as well as negotiation of their clients' investments, whilst certain builders retained tenements as investments, as did widows and spinsters seeking a source of regular income. Lawyers often bought tenements and serviced the needs of the institutions which probably represented the single most important group of owners — the property trusts which administered bequests, inheritances and marriage setttlements.

Legal firms and advisers also developed close contacts with the firms of specialist factors or landlords' agents, responsible for the collection of rents and for dealing with questions of maintenance and tenant complaints in these communally-shared tenement structures. Although the celebrated building firm of the Kennedys managed to retain ownership and factoring in their own hands, as well as building a local railway to transport facing stone to their own construction sites in Partick, their achievement was unusual. Most owners relied upon the quickly growing firms of factors who dealt with almost all matters for a commission upon the rental income, with some factors becoming substantial landlords in their own right as well as managing the property of others and following the areas of new building as far afield as Govan and Clydebank.[30] Since local employers and foremen were reputed to prefer locally settled workmen and occasionally required a reference from the factor, there could develop a mutually reinforcing network of authority in difficult times as landlords avoided letting to unemployed families and local firms were intent on retaining a local pool of available workers. In any case, the practice of demanding substantial deposits and relying upon the testimony of relatives as to family respectability, tended to place the factor (and his clerks) in a powerful and intimate position with many of his tenants.

As in other areas of Scotland, there were three sides of a housing pyramid in Partick which determined access to dwellings: occupation and income; toleration of particular standards and conditions; and physical proximity of both dwellings and work. These forces accounted for the particular distribution of social groups around the Police burgh, with the more attractive northern area descending in gradations of comfort and status to the more primitive working class tenements near the river. Such finer distinctions might be drawn in the quality of tenement 'close' (or main access passage) wall tiles or the painted windows surrounded by varying quality of face stone, though within working class neighbourhoods there existed an alternative hierarchy of preferences and respectability which distinguished individual streets and tenements as superior in attractiveness and standing. Even if the occupational and income distinctions were marked by fairly precise architectural and social boundaries, the real diversity of employment and the very high concentration of skilled journeymen, as well as the accompaniment of migrant cultures and values, gave areas like Partick a peculiar and particular identity in the social life of Clydeside.

The main sources of employment were the shipyards and engineering shops, transport facilities, the building industry itself, and the various distributive and personal services needed to cater for the affluent and local working class groups. Careful local studies have revealed tenements housing building tradesmen alongside engineers, blacksmiths, shipwrights, plumbers and painters, along with motor drivers (commercial, public and chauffeurs) and clerks. With rents ranging from £8 to £18.15s.0d, within individual streets there was again considerable variation in standards and comfort (as well as convenience) within fairly homogeneous working class districts.[31] The fact that districts such as Partick were relatively recent and substantial tenement areas, explains the pattern of housing occupancy, and the steadily improving health and comfort of the inhabitants before 1900. Scottish cities were notorious for their levels of overcrowding, but though a survey of 1911 amongst the poorer of the Partick tenements revealed the overwhelming majority to be of one or two rooms, with wage-earning labourers comprising two-thirds of householders, there were only a handful of actual cases of overcrowding.[32] There was certainly a very high density of people in the burgh, and the figures by Walker Smith and others during Wartime rents enquiries demonstrated the severe shortages of empty housing in such areas after 1910, but both Govan and Partick were characterised by a remarkably high number of substantial and spacious working class tenements inhabited by skilled workers.

Another indication of the relative improvement in both Partick and Govan housing after the 1860s can be taken from the proportions of lower-quality and casual forms of housing provision, ranging from the 'farmed out' furnished dwellings to the common lodging houses which flourished in central Glasgow during the 19th century. Catering mainly for single working men and newly arrived migrants, the lodging houses abounded during the massive influx of workers to the shipbuilding burghs in the 1870s and '80s, with an estimated 700 still operating in 1895 at Partick. Their decline thereafter was dramatic and sustained. As the industrial and building structure of the burghs stabilised, with the impressive new Linthouse development around the Stephen yard in south Govan continuing from the 1870s to 1890s, and an ample supply of tenement accommodation became available, the lower kinds of casual housing were restricted to the casualised and unrespectable groups of labourers. Standards were also driven up by the relentless visits of the Burgh sanitation authorities to suspect tenements, more especially from the 1890s. Originally opposed to the Glasgow practice of 'ticketing', Partick nevertheless increased its urban surveillance until the burgh became one of the healthiest in west Scotland, far outstripping Glasgow in its declining mortality rates as poorer tenements were periodically invaded by vigilant sanitary inspectors.[33] Such testaments to progress were periodically punctuated by the outbreak of epidemics and poverty-induced diseases, as well as by the practice common amongst even highly skilled workers of 'making down' larger flats into smaller units shared by more than one family as economic depression set in.

It is in the relationship between specific examples of improving conditions and the continuation of general housing problems for Glasgow's working population, that we can locate the urban developments of the pre-War years. The consequences of Scotland's peculiar housing tradition had become all too evident by the turn of the century, when the second city of imperial Britain presented the spectacle of magnificent commercial, industrial and municipal buildings within sight of the worst slums that Glasgow possessed.[34] Engels had based his own estimation of the city's housing conditions upon the report of a local sanitary inspector, which had itself contributed to a growing debate on the need for slum clearance in central districts. Local police statutes also regulated the farmed-out houses and common lodging houses in Glasgow proper, (where beds rather than rooms could be rented on a daily basis), as the city authorities moved to reduce the appalling rates of death and disease at the heart of the sprawling metropolis. In 1866 the progressive publishing family of Blackies (only one group amongst a significant minority of urban reformers), were instrumental in forming the City Improvement Trust — responsible for cleaning such verminous plague spots as the old Saltmarket.[35] They were supported by an array of professionals, including medical doctors, academics and evangelising clergymen, anxious to define and resolve the 'housing problem'. In fact, Clydeside experienced not one but three major difficulties in housing its working class during the later 19th century: insanitation, overcrowding and overhousing.

Bad sanitation and overcrowding were particularly marked in the dwellings directly supervised by police inspection. Those houses found to be overcrowded were subject to close scrutiny, with a metal plate or 'ticket' nailed to a door stipulating the maximum number of inhabitants permitted. On the eve of the First World War there were still approximately 22,000 houses (in a total Glasgow stock of perhaps 212,000), 'ticketed' and open to midnight inspection by city police officers.[36] Marginally superior to the 1,500 farmed-out dwellings and common lodging houses, these supervised habitations catered for the needs of the casual and least skilled workers' families pressed below the poverty line. Inspectors from the slum districts of Cowcaddens or Gorbals had little to learn from the London experiences of Mearns and Solly.[37]

Standards and impressions of overcrowding varied between different parts of Britain, but there were very few areas to equal the sheer density of settlement and population which affected the bulk of Glasgow's working class. In 1902, for example, Professor Smart of Glasgow University estimated that about 23% of occupied houses (or 36,000 households), consisted of one room 'single ends', and another 45% (or 70,000 families and occupants) carried on family life in two apartments.[38] In 1915, it was more accurately calculated that well over 70% of Glasgow housing comprised one or two rooms, which itself represented a considerable deterioration since 1911.[39] At the same time there had existed a substantial surplus of housing which indicated to some writers the problems of 'overhousing', with 14,000 larger dwellings (of two or three rooms) standing empty in 1913. The fact that much fewer single ends were available to working people suggests the underlying problems of insufficient demand for better accommodation and larger houses, itself caused by the low levels of real income and inability (or unwillingness) to pay higher rents demanded for such property.[40] Even the more affluent skilled workers often preferred to begin married life in a one room tenement flat, before progressing to larger dwellings with families and 'doubling up' with other households in periods of unemployment.[41] Where landlords were still insisting on annual letting of better properties, retained by a sizeable deposit in advance, skilled tradesmen could not commit their families in the troughs of 1903-08. Even for those able and willing to rent larger flats, workers continued to pay for elaborate structure and building overheads rather than living space, in contrast to their English counterparts. As the building industry stagnated on low profits, the options available were steadily deteriorating.

The pressure of impersonal economic forces was expressed in alternative cultural forms during the pre-War decades, ranging from denunciation of unreliable tenants by propertied interests to the growing insistence on better housing at this period, objective conditions being described and examined in highly moralistic terms. The Glasgow Municipal Commission on Housing which sat for two years from 1902, combined statistical analysis with sweeping generalisation on the minority of vicious loafers and criminals amongst those inhabiting ticketed dwellings.[42] They delivered an interesting appraisal of workers in irregular employment and the 'substantial leavening of skilled men earning better wages', who were to be found in the farmed out houses or lodging dens but introduced ambivalent distinctions of 'respectability' at the same time. One significant development after the 1870s was the growing professionalisation of the housing problem in Glasgow, as various experts from the medical profession, local government, universities, legal practice and religious and philanthropic institutions, sought to define the limits of the 'problem' more accurately. Although such professions usually had some interest in the preservation of general property and authority relations within Scottish society, there arose an autonomous critique of housing conditions at Glasgow and elsewhere before the War. It is significant that many such reports and enquiries by expert observers translate the dominant cultural values of the 19th century into the language of scientific investigation. Thus Peter

Fyfe, Glasgow's Sanitary Inspector, wrote as late as 1916, that:[43]

The question of the provision of houses for artisans and their families, and people of equal status, is differentiated from the same question in connection with that class of population which is beneath them in the social order, and who are usually designated under the term 'the poorer classes'... the class of casual and other unskilled labourers beneath them.

Those professionals who joined the ranks of the radical and socialist societies or parties were more forthright than Professor Smart or Peter Fyfe, but they also assimilated a strong ethical appeal in their analysis. It was against many cultural traditions and religious prejudices that pioneering reformers such as John Wheatley and Andrew McBride had to struggle at the turn of the century. Thus Bruce Glasier had testified to the Presbytery Commission on Housing in 1890 that the Irish were amongst the least skilled and worst housed sections of the population, lacking both craft and union protection.[44] Divisions in the labour market along sectarian and religious lines helps to explain the toleration of relative deprivation by many skilled men concentrated in particular neighbourhoods, and the effective repression of resistance in the well-policed slum districts.

These are unmistakable signs that this cultural hegemony — and its definition of housing conditions amongst working people — was under threat before the War. Ideas of legitimate property ownership and management were always subject to challenges and resistance during the 19th century, whether by an immigrant and dispossessed rural labour force (with their own bitter memories of landlord rights and evictions), or from skilled workers removing without the factors' consent.[45] Individual responsibility for rent arrears and house maintenance was also difficult in the shared experience of the tenement close. Perhaps the greatest enemy of landlord influence was this *enforced collectivity* of Glasgow housing: beyond the crowded apartments lay the communal water closets, back court wash-houses, collectively-scrubbed close stairs, and even common water supply. Unlike recent high-density housing for working families, the eight or twelve dwellings of the Victorian tenement imposed a direct contact with neighbours which involved complaints or notice of repairs to the factor and a mutual respect for basic standards of behaviour. An individual close acquired a particular identity and atmosphere which affected all its inhabitants, and more specifically the women who spent their working day and night in sight of a shared washing line. It is this very concentration of families in one or two rooms, coupled with a strong sexual division of labour, which contributed to the persistent absence of adult males (frequently engaged in physically exhausting manual labour for nine or ten hours) from the household. Men created a powerful tradition of hard drinking and outdoor sports, reinforced by religious allegiance and membership of Orange, Hibernian or Masonic societies.[46] Similarly, there continued a rich custom of public speaking and debate on religious, political and public issues at Glasgow Green and elsewhere, influencing the generation of activists which arose in the pre-War years.[47]

The antagonisms and frustrations, as much as the sense of shared experience, surfaced more powerfully after the 1890s. Owners and factors strove to ensure that their tenants should pay economical rents and continue occupancy for a fixed period, whilst Glasgow Corporation sought to rationalise its administration and rating system by amalgamating surrounding burghs such as Govan, Partick and Rutherglen and compounding various police and house rates in a charge to factors. Burghs such as Govan insisted on years of immunity from Glasgow charges as the price of their absorption into the Corporation, whilst a host of ratepaying groups (covering lower middle class as well as working class tenants) emerged in the decade before the War. The assortment of Liberals, Independents, 'Stalwarts' and local careerists who had dominated Glasgow municipality with a significant degree of government intervention during the 1890s, were confronted with the mobilisation of ratepaying voters upon a range of social questions.[48] As early as 1902, I.L.P. candidates were appealing to 'small shopkeepers who have to keep up upon a small income a decent appearance', and who were adversely affected by rates and rent increases.[49] These lesser propertied and professional groups were themselves divided in interest and outlook, many being owners and investors in working class housing whilst others faced heavy burdens of rents and rates at their shop or business premises. Numerous educated and professional individuals supported the resurgent socialist movement at Glasgow, though others joined bodies such as the Glasgow Protective Association under Lewis.[50] These forces shared a powerful critique of landed and rentier profits, partly inspired by Georgeism and woven into a more sustained attack on capitalist production itself.

The most obvious indication of a mounting conflict between landlords and tenants appears in the rising tide of evictions and contested actions in pre-War Glasgow.[51] Yet the more vocal campaign revolved around the issue of letting and rating conditions in the city. This grievance had become more evident during the unemployment distress of 1907-08, and possibly also after the appearance of large numbers of empty flats which offered lower rents than those occupied by many families. Following the sitting and report of the Guthrie Committee on this problem in Glasgow, the Government legislated for reduction of lets in the House Letting and Rating Act. Unfortunately for the tenants, this was implemented to the landlords' advantage as shortages of accommodation replaced uneven surpluses and as landlords began to compound rates in such a way that increases could be hidden beneath a general police and public rates charge. It was in response to the introduction of this Act that tenants' organisations received a great momentum, with local ward committees in areas such as Govan and Fairfield setting up Tenants' Defence Associations.[52] In 1913 David Wardley and the Govan T.D.A. approached local M.P.s on the question of rents and rates, no doubt voicing the common complaint that landlords' agents were cheating the tenants of 'factors' odd coppers' and requested the introduction of local rents tribunals.[53] The Letting and Rating Act also allowed landlords to raise rents and demand ejectments by the month (as against the year), in areas such as Govan or Partick where the growth of shipbuilding workforces placed enormous pressures on available housing. This may well account for continued rise in court actions over ejectments before the outbreak of War, and the determined legal resistance by the tenants.

Legal obligations and Tenant resistance

Within a libertarian legal tradition, which permitted the elected Baillies of Scottish burghs to serve as local magistrates, tenants were able to develop various strategies of resistance which made the judicial system a particularly important area of class conflict at this period. Assisted by radical and socialist advocates, such as Rosslyn Mitchell, their delaying tactics allowed the critics of landlordism to formulate and defend a coherent programme of housing reform in the course of opposing ejectments or rent rises. It was in this context that the central demand for Fair Rents Courts or rents tribunals was persistently pressed home by the various sections of the anti-landlord movement, becoming by the outbreak of the War the 'old annual' to an unsympathetic press.[54] The concept of a 'fair' as against a 'free' rent attracted a support never achieved by the advocates of 'fair trade' amongst working people, representing an important challenge to prevailing legal notions of property rights and freedom of contract.

To understand the political significance of alternative values on the fairness of landlord behaviour and local government proposals, it is vital to appreciate the local particularisms in which urban politics were usually phrased as well as the existence of autonomous working class institutions which offered different ethics of contractual obligations than those of private business. It was only on the eve of War that Partick and Govan were fully integrated into the municipal system of Glasgow government, though each had developed a distinctive style of local politics during the later 19th century and like Glasgow relied upon local police legislation as the basis of their burgh administration. The Glasgow Police Acts of 1891-92 were in some respects as significant as the Housing of the Working Classes legislation of 1890, in empowering local authorities to regulate housing conditions more stringently. Burgh politics were less openly politicised than in the city itself before the 1900s, though both Govan and Partick were heavily influenced by the three constraints of property relationships, religious divisions, and the growth of a distinct labour presence in burgh affairs during the last quarter of the 19th century. It is hard to accept the view of some writers that districts such as Partick were depoliticised by the tone of evangelising morality that coloured local affairs, even if a fairly tightly-knit urban bourgeoisie effectively retained power during the pre-War years against the challenge of outsiders.[55] The fact that such local provosts and baillies were prepared to sponsor relief funds and voluntary bodies such as the Partick Civic Guild in these years, suggests a growing recognition of the need for fresh responses to familiar problems of cyclical unemployment and endemic poverty. The Partick Civic Guild praised the benevolence of factors who did not press their claims for rent arrears in the difficult years of unemployment, but also responded to arguments in favour of deserving tenants faced with depression.[56]

Popular cultures and social provision

There are both contrasts and similarities in the growth of Govan and Partick which help to explain the relatively stronger support which Labour was to enjoy in the former district. Govan was an older and more established industrial district, with an even clearer focus upon shipbuilding and related engineering work than Partick. Building was still going on in south Govan and near the yards in the 1890s, but its formative years were past and the landscape was well established by the time the Elders and Pearces provided parks and institutes in the 1870s-'90s. There were noticeably poorer areas of housing inhabited by labourers and casual workers, such as the tenements near the Graving Dock and where immigrant Irish and Highland workers found accommodation.[57] Whereas Partick was a youthful area of substantial tenements and recent generations of immigrants, Govan had both a longer history and stronger identity as a working class locality. Although the institutions of organised labour were beginning to surface in Partick, with its high proportion of unionised craft workers, it did not possess the equivalent of Govan Trades Council nor the network of A.S.E. and Boilermakers' membership that the south side of the River enjoyed. Equally important, perhaps, the occupational composition and social character of Partick was much more ambiguous, situated as it was between the great commercial centre of Glasgow and the shipyards of Whiteinch and Scotstoun down river. Its northern area contained one of the most prestigious residential districts of suburban Glasgow, which provided important employment for numerous men and (more importantly) women in servicing the larger houses and flats, as well as dominating Police Burgh affairs from the 1850s. Middle class philanthropy and religion was much more evident and influential in Partick than the Presbytery of Govan could hope to be in the staunchly proletarian and free-drinking streets of its parish.

Popular attitudes to religion did acquire powerful political significance in both burghs, richly provided as each was with the carnivals of Roman Catholicism and

Orangeism from the mid-century years. Govan witnessed the procession of football crowds to nearby Ibrox every other weekend, as well as the more explicitly Orange Protestant celebrations of July 12th, though it was Partick which probably had the more recent concentrations of Ulster Orangemen who migrated to the shipyards later taken over by the Belfast firm of Harland & Wolff. Ulster skilled workers were still arriving during the labour shortages of the First World War, probably relying upon a network of local connections to secure them accommodation and social recreation in the hard-pressed burgh. Whereas in Govan, Catholics and Protestants were able to preserve a tolerable distance by settling in distinctive areas (reinforced by the occupational and social divisions uncovered by the 1890 Presbytery Commission on housing), the very concentration and density of Partick's urban growth pressed them into uncomfortable proximity around Partick Cross and Dumbarton Road. Whilst burgh politics was never directly infected by open sectarian contests, there is little doubt that propertied groups maintained an indulgent disregard for discrimination and violence against Roman Catholics, as during the sectarian rioting of 1875.[58]

Amongst the authentic working class institutions which both Govan and Partick possessed by the end of the century, was the cooperative society. Like friendly societies, cooperative stores involved far more people in membership and regular participation than did trade unions and were certainly more well known amongst women responsible for maintaining the household economy. The societies also represented an alternative set of principles and practices to profit-making enterprises such as the Govan Victualling Society, even if most customers were far more interested in the thrift accumulation entailed in dividends than the annual general meetings. Even in their everyday trading practices, the cooperatives were something more than appendage to market capitalism or a limited exercise in socialist shopkeeping. The later leader of rent strikes and Labour councils, Patrick Dollan, was to claim a particular eminence for the Kinning Park Society, noting in his 1923 history, that:[59]

The history of working-class politics is interwoven with the evolution of the Society, which has done more than most

societies to educate the workers to realise the possibilities of wise action in politics.

Dollan suggested that the very early days of the Society were marked by pioneering political activity on behalf of working men, with ward elections for each of the four wards occupied by K.P.C.S. premises becoming 'a genuine conflict between artisans and employers for control of the burgh'.[60] It is more realistic to recognise the importance of land reform issues in Scottish urban politics during the 1880s, which the Society supported as a contribution to the recreation of a radical alliance which was not specifically proletarian in its outlook. With cooperative backing, Shaw Maxwell was able to record a respectable vote of 1,200 for the Land Restoration League at Blackfriars during the 1880s.[61]

Another important locus for cooperative influence and progressive agitation during the 1880s were the elections to local School Boards, such as the Govan Board upon which shipbuilders such as Alexander Stephen served. Kinning Park activists began promoting working men as popular candidates, making education elections one of the most political of local government contests after a long quiescence in the responsible government of their superiors.[62] After affiliating to the Scottish Workers' Representative Committee, the Society openly supported the principle of greater labour representation in municipal government as well as upon key agencies of social administration such as the School Boards.[63] Following the annexation of Partick and Govan to Glasgow in 1913, there occurred the municipal elections which carried Andrew Welsh to City Chambers as Cooperative candidate along with John Taylor, and in 1913 they were joined by prominent I.L.P.ers, Denny, Dollan and Wardley — all members of the Kinning Park Society.[64] The cooperatives were clearly one of the most important connection networks in the building of the new Labour coalition at Glasgow and elsewhere.

Yet the cooperative movement and its advocates were not free from ambiguous commitments in the handling of even the most fundamental questions of landed property and participation of their membership in society affairs. In districts such as Partick and Govan, the cooperatives figured as owners of a number of tenements, usually housing their employees, though presumably also purchased along with substantial ground floor premises for their retail activities. The ambivalence in their attitudes towards property ownership is implicit in Dollan's remark that by the late 19th century, the Kinning Park body was a substantial landlord, 'and could no longer be sneered at by provincials because it was without property'.[65] Public respectability and acceptance was seen as turning on the ownership and control of real estate in key areas, even if Dollan goes on to defend the generous renting and factoring practices of the society as landlords.[66] At the same time, Kinning Park invited the chairman of the local I.L.P., W. C. Anderson (prominent as M.P. for Attercliffe and defender of rent strikers later), to give a lecture on municipal politics, during which he outlined a bold policy for 'the abolition of the slums and their replacement by cottage homes'.[67] The cooperatives were increasingly aligned with the progressive forces on housing and other questions, but were themselves entangled in property relations and prevailing attitudes despite an alternative vision of trade and politics.

Equally remarkable was the attitude which many societies adopted towards working class women, who formed the overwhelming majority of their customers and dividend holders. Housewives and other labouring women were much less prominent in the management and government of the societies than in their own form of shop floor bargaining across cooperative counters. The formation of Cooperative Women's Guilds in the late 19th century did give women their own ancillary organisations, capable of attracting women of widely differing personal and political interests, though without articulating any decidedly feminist programme. It is an indication of a certain form of conservatism amongst active cooperators, that women should have been noticeably excluded from the foundation ceremony for a new cooperative building in 1891, where it was 'not considered good form for women to appear on the platform at Cooperative or other working-class meetings'. After subsequent protests by the Cooperative Guilds, they were invited to participate in such public celebrations of success, but were again less influential in the conduct of society business than the personal management of household consumption.[68]

The struggles of local cooperators and their societies to come to terms with general codes of behaviour and belief, as well as a changing world of political issues do not reveal so much their limitations as the difficulties of reappraising the conventional terms in which politics were expressed.

Encountering debates on landed wealth and taxation, such societies as the Govan-based K.P.C.S., moved towards a more distinctly labour perspective though still perceiving this in terms of government representation. They remained primarily concerned with maintaining decent standards of efficiency and integrity as societies, whilst engaging in political and educational campaigns on housing and other questions. In order to appreciate the contribution they made to working people's everyday attitudes, we have to look at both general and particular developments in working class politics and the contacts made between activists in different campaigns. One of the most important initiatives in this regard, were those struggles which cumulatively politicised the women's question in the years before the War.

CHAPTER THREE

Women and the progress of working class politics before the War

Whilst working class women were the group most directly affected by any inadequacy in housing conditions, their ability to organise on this and other issues was seriously constrained by their customary role in industry and society. Recruitment to trade unions amongst women was proceeding steadily but undramatically before 1914, reinforcing the less formal methods of workplace restriction practised by women in such trades as textile production in west Scotland. Mary Macarthur and Margaret Bondfield promoted the Federation of Women Workers at Glasgow as well as English industrial centres, though they achieved limited success until the outbreak of War began to radically alter the structure of the workforce and the attitudes of female workers. Yet it would be wrong to assume that women were completely hidden in the history of workplace struggle, or their initiatives obscured from the trade union movement. During the great waves of unrest that accompanied the strike campaigns at London and the provinces, women participated in conflicts from the campaigns of the London match girls to the Lancashire textile workers, to improve their status and remuneration in the world of labour.

In the spread of industrial strikes during the pre-War years, women figured along with male-dominated occupations such as coalmining, railway transportation and dockland trades, in the culmination of what many respectable observers saw as the crisis of Liberal society. In the west of Scotland dyeing district of the Vale of Leven (later to become celebrated as a 'Little Moscow' stronghold under Communist influence), women were mobilising before the War, as they were in the trouble-torn districts of South Wales and areas of London itself. In 1912, the central committee of the Independent Labour Party, which had been born out of the Manningham protests involving women and men workers, told its assembled delegates that:[69]

On the industrial side it may be recorded that the women workers have been active in the brave struggles of the past twelve months. . . . The widespread character of the Labour unrest amongst women is proved by the fact that there were women's strikes at St. Pancras, Clerkenwell, Ware . . . Swansea, Leith and Vale of Leven.

Women in such declining textile centres such as Partick also continued to play an important role in a variety of public activities, even if some of these lacked the approval of sober society. Sectarian religious contests had seen women amongst the most bitter opponents, with one newspaper commenting of the 1875 religious riot in the Partick area, that 'the wild and fierce energy displayed by a large number of women who took an active part in the affray', was one of its resounding features.[70]

It was in the pre-War period itself, however, that the political significance of women's civil and social status came to prominence as a major question for the organised working class as well as the powerful of Edwardian Society. The relationship between the emerging suffragist movement and mainstream political organisations of working people, as well as the connections between middle class feminists and the organisers of women's trade unions, remained difficult and uneasy for much of the pre-War era. Divisions became apparent during and after the formation of the Women's Social and Political Union in 1906, and its almost immediate intervention in parliamentary politics by contesting bye-elections at Huddersfield (in the heart of I.L.P territory) and scenic Cockermouth. Focussing solely on the issue of female emancipation, the W.S.P.U. issued a manifesto which brought it into direct conflict with the claims of the Independent Labour Party. These and other controversial questions were debated at the 1907 conference of the Party, where the National Administrative Council observed the support which it had received from 'distinctively Women's Labour Organisations', such as the Women's Labour League, in its attempts to make the progressive case in bye-elections.[71]

Further rancour accompanied the discussion of the proposal to send telegrams of congratulation and support to women suffragists who had been imprisoned for violent tactics of direct action in support of their campaigns, with Bruce Glasier of Glasgow and Mrs MacDonald strongly resisting the motion. Whilst suggesting that such tactics reflected a particular kind of martyrdom, he reserved his commendation for those women who had stood faithfully by the cause of Labour, and he remained 'for the women's cause, but not for the Women's Political Union'.[72] The conference finally voted to adopt Keir Hardie's suggestion that they send telegrams as a graceful gesture, and by 1909 the Party was denouncing prison sentences passed upon 500 women who figured in the current agitation, as vindictive and excessive.[73] There were still important criticisms of the I.L.P and Labour attitude towards the women's questions, such as the Liberal treatment of workless females and the unjust application of the Unemployed Workmen's Act of 1905.[74] Caroline Despard of Battersea raised such issues as the inadequate provision of workrooms for women in the metropolis, and in 1910 joined with Mrs Arnot Robinson in a general attack on the I.L.P. leadership for its supine neglect of the suffrage question, whilst another speaker reminded the conference that:[75]

Socialism included the question of Women's Suffrage, and they should do all in their power to retain the enthusiasms of their women and not commit the mistake made by other sections of the Socialist Movement in this country.

In such debates the embers of past antagonisms were raked over, with one feminist speaker insisting at a 1913 conference that the frictions of 1906 had forced Mrs Pankhurst's departure from the I.L.P., with the suffragists 'sent out . . . to fight their own battles'.[76] In the bitter exchanges which followed, George Lansbury and his feminist supporters from Poplar figured, with Lansbury arguing for a deletion of any reference to the Union of Suffrage Societies as the 'most influential' section of the franchise campaign. Further tension followed W. C. Anderson's correction (from the chair), that any financial support had been forthcoming from the National Union, in which he firmly denied any such assistance had been given — though the money collected by women 'who were fighting for their freedom was as clean and honest as any that could come from any section of the community'.[77]

The renewed friction between the Labour activists and the most vigorous sections of the suffrage movement came over the question of acceptable tactics and the use of force. Dr. Marion Phillips of Kensington rose to refute the case made by Lansbury, in a speech clearly informed by the nuances of metropolitan politics as well as her personal experience of suffrage struggle. She emphatically denied the suggestion that militancy had forwarded the cause of reform, despite the sensational interest of newspapers in the incidents of violence, and argued that the National Union should not be associated with such extreme elements, noting that:[78]

Militant action had switched the thoughts of the people off Suffrage and on to mere discussions of violence, and had aroused in people's minds a feeling of exasperation and aggravation, which would not help the women's cause. . . . The militants had ceased to do Suffrage work, and were merely carrying on methods of violence.

Dr. Phillips had left the National Union because she felt that the proper place for socialist and Labour women was 'inside their own organisation, and not in a separate one'.[79] Such decisions were made against the background of constitutional crisis and Conservative gains in the elections of 1910, with popular support for Toryism in resurgence alongside industrial unrest at home and troubles in Ulster.

Beyond London itself, however, the contingents of working class women amongst the W.S.P.U. membership appear to have remained resilient despite the open hostility often expressed by national industrial leaders to the suffrage campaigns. In Glasgow, for example, there were close links between W.S.P.U. activities and prominent women I.L.P.ers such as Helen Crawfurd, the daughter of a prosperous Gorbals baker and wife of a socialist clergyman from the Anderston slum district.[80] As in the 1840s and 1870s, the ability of progressives to secure the support of important sections of the local clergy was to contribute an impressive element of moral force along with more prosaic alternatives to prevailing political economy, in the struggle to create a fresh coalition of radical campaigners. Suffragists were quite capable of making their own approaches to organised labour, however, and in 1912 the Glasgow Trades Council heard the arguments of three women on the case for reform, though the skilled engineering delegates argued that adult suffrage for all should be their policy rather than parity within an unequal franchise.[81]

Various connections were made between women's issues and the housing question in these years of controversy, ranging from an explicit identification of women's special interest in the subject of domestic comfort and decency to the advocacy of home-based tactics in the struggle for wider questions of change. One of the most novel suggestions for the involvement of housewives and rentpayers in the feminist movement came from Sylvia Pankhurst's section of the London suffrage organisations, proposing as they did the formation of a 'People's Army' under the command of the East London Federation of Suffragettes to resist police brutality and to implement a 'No Vote No Rent Strike' in the deprived areas of the capital. Taking their initiative from the radical tenant resistance already evident in the East End, the E.L.F.S. were able to popularise their campaign so effectively that Glasgow's Labour weekly carried a report before the War.[82]

In another context, women active in the I.L.P. raised the general question of decent accommodation for single or unattached females in the major cities and the lack of facilities comparable to the lodging houses patronised by homeless or migrant males. Mrs Ayles told the 1911 conference of the I.L.P. of the difficulties faced by charwomen, hop-pickers and other women workers in cities such as Bristol and Birmingham trying to find a safe and respectable lodgings. In urging local authorities to provide municipal lodging houses to cater for this group of workers, she pointed out that:[83]

At present the only safe place to go was the casual ward [of the Workhouse] or the ordinary common lodging house, these were not pleasant places for women to have to spend the night.

This was a problem which was to return with a vengeance during the industrial shortages of 1915-16, as a desperate government sought to secure accommodation for key munitions workers in areas where hostels for women were overcrowded or unknown.

More significant for their engagement of women working at home or in different kinds of domestic service near their neighbourhoods, were the various tenant campaigns and organisations which sprang up in areas such as Clydeside during the pre-War years. Tenants' Defence associations had both men and women in positions of responsibility, though the housewives tended to figure as the day to day activists. Such campaigns depended upon a series of connections built up through local consumer facilities, particularly the local cooperative societies and ancillary associations. Amongst the patrons of the Kinning Park Society in Govan, were housewives such as Mrs Mary Barbour of South Govan, along with George Buchanan, Emmanuel Shinwell and other prominent I.L.P.ers.[84] David Wardley was another member prominent in the Society's development, who also joined with Mrs Barbour and others in promoting tenant organisations in Fairfield and other Govan districts. Such bodies as the Tenants' Defence Association and other Govan Women's Housing Association developed programmes which went beyond the mere defence of local interests in calling for a radical reshaping of working class housing at municipal level, though it was due to local activists such as Mary Barbour (lifelong member of the Labour Party and feminist campaigner on such issues as education and birth control) that the tenant issues were transformed into the everyday politics of the immediate area.[85] Married to a Fairfield shipyard engineer and able to rely upon widespread support in the Govan area, Mrs Barbour was later to become a Labour councillor — ironically by defeating David Wardley in a Fairfield ward divided by personal differences in post-War Clydeside — and the first woman Baillie in Glasgow.[86] Dollan was even to claim in 1923 that the rent strikes of 1915 began amongst the Kinning Park Society activists in South Govan, who refused to pay an increase of 3s.1d. per month and persuaded others to do likewise until restrictions were imposed, and in this respect the Society was a true benefactor of 'consumers outwith as well as within the movement'.[87] Whether or not this was true, the integration of organisational membership certainly assisted the mobilisation of women against landlords during the resistance movements of the pre-War and War years.

Another prominent Labour activist and patron of the Women's Labour League was Mary B. Laird, founding member and first president of the Glasgow Women's Housing Association which was formed on the eve of War itself. Both the Labour League and the Housing Committee of the Glasgow Labour Party (established by Andrew McBride in 1913), were instrumental in the creation of the Glasgow Women's Housing Association, though again the new organisation was formally non-political in its membership and commitments. The secretary of the Labour Party at Glasgow and a regular contributor to the Labour paper *Forward,* Ben Shaw, was to write of a conference organised by the Glasgow Women's Housing Association and sponsored by the I.L.P. in early 1915, that:[88]

Housing is, above all, a woman's question. Women have already enough votes and influence to turn the balance in favour of the Labour Party — which is the only Housing Party. . . . If every ill-housed woman who cherises a housing ambition can be brought to demand it fiercely, and collectively, its realisation will be assured.

The Housing Association's first president emphasised the moral texture of working class life and the urgent need for an organisation such as theirs to campaign for municipal housing free of interest payments.[89] The women speakers agreed with Labour spokesmen such as Patrick Dollan, Andrew McBride and John Wheatley that only State intervention could remedy the terminal decline in the housebuilding industry at Clydeside and elsewhere.

Other collective organisations contributed to a mobilisation of women on the housing and other social issues, with the Women's Labour League providing such talented recruiting officers as Mrs Ferguson and Mrs Nixon, who promoted the formation of housing associations in each ward of the city and affiliated to the Glasgow Women's Housing Association. The Women's Freedom League shared a district organiser with the W.L.L. for a period at this time, claiming a strong presence in the Springburn area where the wives of skilled engineers attended kitchen meetings to discuss general matters of political importance.[90] Probably more conservative in their membership and outlook were the Cooperative Women's Guilds, which (according to Dollan) cleared the roads to freedom along which women 'were to march to a higher and nobler status life'.[91] Yet they seem to have included a substantial number of traditionalist and even Orangeist supporters in their ranks, though strong in the defence of living standards and neighbourhood conditions.[92] The participation of such diverse and divergent groups of women during the housing campaigns and consumer movements may help to explain the strongly ethical and patriotic terms in which Wartime crusades were phrased, as well as the broad support which I.L.P. activists were able to command on such questions. Such a resurgence of protest amongst Glasgow women was undoubtedly more appealing for its broad political complexion and the attempts to elaborate political initiatives from the lifestyles and customs familiar to housewives rather than by imposing a framework of central direction.

CHAPTER FOUR

The Independent Labour Party and the Housing Question

The growing influence which the Independent Labour Party and the Labour coalition in general appeared to enjoy from the 1890s, has to be explained mainly in terms of its ability to accommodate a variety of issues and autonomous interests within the terms of socialist politics. The appearance and ascendancy of an independent Labour voice was a departure of real importance which involved the transformation of popular politics in distinct areas of the country, integrating different bodies in the challenge to the Liberal constituency. Whilst it would be misleading to see this in terms of a reflex to the employers' offensives of the 1890s, the I.L.P. did assemble a set of industrial policies intended to appeal to the main forces of organised labour, as well as developing programmes in response to feminist issues, tenants' and housing campaigns, and broader constitutional or social reforms. It is against this background of an uneven progress of distinct issues that we can locate the significance of the housing question for working class politics before the War.

It was the appropriate attitude which working class organisations should adopt towards socialism and socialists that occupied many of the early debates within the Independent Labour Party. Trade unions were recognised as the authentic expression of working class aspirations at the workplace, though the connection between trade unionism and what Tillett called 'the best sort of Socialism and Labourism', became a source of controversy from the early days of the Party. In making his case for the development of a politicised labour movement which would build upon the achievements of native trade unionism rather than Continental or internationalist socialism, telling an early conference that:[93]

He wished to capture the trades' unionists of this country, a body of men well organised who paid their money and were Socialists at their work every day and not merely on the platform . . .

Tillett's brave faith in British working men must have been damaged somewhat when the Trade Union Congress decided in 1895 to restrict access to the Congress by unaffiliated groups of socialists. The leadership of the I.L.P. reaffirmed its belief in the forward march to international socialism of British labour, though the party did not concentrate its energies (as later syndicalist parties were to do) on the promotion of workplace struggle, before the War.[94] Rather it would seem that I.L.P. activists were also prominent on local trades councils and amongst local branches of key trades unions, as John S. Taylor and Harry Hopkins of the A.S.E. were to be at Govan on Clydeside. It was also at Govan that John Hill of the Boilermakers' Society received the nomination as Labour candidate in the 1906 general election, supported by the cooperative vote as well as key industrial organisations and local councillors.[95]

The industrial unrest of the immediate pre-War years appears to have had an uneven impact upon the fortunes of organised labour, as the political appeal of the Labour Party declined in key areas such as Lancashire and even London, though the I.L.P. did confront the Liberal government with the handling of industrial troubles. Strongly criticising the Tory demands for a repeal of the 1906 Trade Disputes Act, the 1912 conference of the I.L.P. at Merthyr also condemned the Asquith administration's provocative drafting of troops into major industrial centres during the railway strike. It warned the Liberals that:[96]

The responsibility for the shooting, wounding, and killing that took place at Liverpool and Llanelly lies at the door of the Government. The remedy for Labour unrest is not soldiers and special constables nor the repeal of the Trade Disputes Act, but the granting of justice to the workpeople.

It was the I.L.P. which enrolled many of the key shop stewards who were to figure in the Wartime labour troubles in areas such as Clydeside, even if the rival Socialist Labour Party did establish a powerful presence at plants such as Singer's of Clydebank before being dispersed across the region following an unsuccessful pre-War strike.

One area where municipal programmes and industrial policies came together, was in the efforts of various Glasgow I.L.P.ers to impose a minimum wage upon all those having contracts with the Corporation. In early 1914, councillor John Wheatley moved that the municipal authorities should only give contracts to firms paying a minimum wage of 25s. per week, which was resisted by the Town Clerk who encouraged protests from the coalowners supplying the Corporation, amongst others.[97] The coal-masters informed the authorities that such a motion being carried would preclude them from tendering for supplies of fuel to the Corporation, even though the coal employers were facing strong union pressure to improve wages and conditions in the west Scotland fields before the War.[98] Such initiatives helped to sustain the tentative connections being made between industrial and political questions, as expressed in the 1912 I.L.P. call for 'both industrial and political unity', as well as the distinct areas of housing campaigns and party programmes before the war.[99]

This involved the elaboration of the Labour platform on municipal reform and its particular emphasis on housing problems in districts such as Clydeside, though much of the early impetus to legislative proposals came from London itself. In 1900 I.L.P.ers heard J. F. Green of the City branch, outline a comprehensive housing strategy which included provisions for compulsory purchase of land, directives to clear slum sites, government loans and the rating and taxation of vacant land, as well as the introduction of Fair Rents Courts and the right of householders to make representations on housing needs. The additional demand for the public registration of all land and houseowners reflected a keen awareness of the continuing power of urban propertied interests, and the need for greater participation of tenants in the administration of housing by local authorities.[100] When the I.L.P. met in the notoriously slum-ridden city of Liverpool in 1902, Snowden seconded a motion to meet the dual problems of overcrowding and high rents by borrowing money at low interest from savings banks and the extension of local government powers to acquire land for developing 'municipal housing estates'.[101] Such motions were increasingly informed by a wider debate upon the architecture and design of urban and suburban estates, associated with Patrick Geddes as well as Ebenezer Howard.[102]

There were also periodic criticisms of those Labour notables who had entered Liberal government but put their official powers to little effective use, as when John Burns's town planning measure of 1908 was denounced as 'the most colossal endowment of landlordism seen in the present generation', by Snowden.[103] There were also divisions over the extent of municipal involvement and reform required, as when John S. Taylor of Govan (seconding Mrs Reeves) was opposed in his call for a special committee to investigate the whole question of municipal rating and an alternative motion from F. W. Jowett passed.[104] The progressives returned to their crusade for special emphasis on the housing issue when in 1914 they called for the creation of a National Housing Council to collect and disseminate information on the housing question. In rejecting a continued reliance upon the Local Government Information Bureau under the joint aegis of I.L.P. and Fabian Society, the advocates of the Council insisted that a body was needed which would 'guide the policy of the local I.L.P. Councillors', as well as providing them with precise local and technical information on different proposals.[105] Such initiatives towards greater organisation and information gathering were being made in the Glasgow context and elsewhere, and it is interesting that the Party should have conceived of a national council in terms of servicing local councillors rather than providing a central policy-making forum as such.

Another general theme which emerges from the growing interest in the housing question during the pre-War years is the socialist vision of the future generation and the particular place accorded to the world of childhood as well as the secure environment of a decent home. So in 1911 the conference of the I.L.P. recognised the creative contribution which local authorities could make not only in dealing with housing and unemployment, but in advancing 'the Education and the Medical Inspection, Feeding and Surgical or Medical Treatment of children'.[106] Youth and childhood were especially significant periods of development for the builders of the future society, and organisations such as the I.L.P. were able to promote a fresh culture of collective recreation and healthy exercise which included the support of 2,500 'Cycle Scouts' who were encouraged to disseminate socialist literature in the rural districts as well as enjoying the countryside.[107] The imagery of domestic deprivation and family oppression was also to be found in the hymns and songs of the Socialist Sunday Schools established in west Scotland and elsewhere before the First World War. Enjoyment of the countryside figured alongside the vision of the new Jerusalem and the Golden City which would replace the depressing urban landscape of industrial capitalism.[108] Popular culture in Scotland seems to have been particularly influenced by such activities, which coloured the rhetoric of the housing delegates as well as the appeals of Hardie and others for a distinctive ethical understanding of social issues behind the programmes of practical change.

It was therefore in this rich and complex world of changing relationships that the outlook and political convictions of working people were expressed and developed. The boundaries of legitimate politics were being broadened and redrawn as State intervention at both local and central levels expanded after the 1880s. The group of ideas and philosophies often classified under the title of 'municipal socialism' often followed, rather than preceded, local initiatives and it was from the combination of practical reforms as well as political discourse that we can trace the growing support for housing improvement as well as Labour politics. Thus Glasgow had become by the 1900s the most municipalised city in Britain under the influence of ruling Liberals and Independents.[109] From 1897, however, there was a persistent pressure from Labour 'stalwarts', after a Glasgow workers' Municipal Committee was set up to bring together trades unions, Glasgow Trades Council, cooperative movement, I.L.P., United Irish League and the Social Democratic Federation, behind a coherent platform of municipal reforms.[110] The participation of the Irish League was to be particularly important in bridging the gulf between Home Rulers and other Labour causes as well as between Roman Catholicism and Scottish socialism.

Undoubtedly the most powerful element in this alliance was the I.L.P., which acted with local Labour Representation Associations to provide a broad umbrella for autonomous organisations in social and political life. The I.L.P. *was* the 'Labour Party' on the ground and in constituency wards around Clydeside, with a very diverse and rich life of socialist debate within its ranks — ranging from the ethical socialism inspired by religious backgrounds and free thought philosophy to the rigorous analysis of capitalism in Scotland provided by Wheatley, Thomas Johnston and Maxton. It was this moral appeal against the degradation and indecency imposed by the private housing market that allowed local canvassers to strengthen the appeal of the I.L.P. in the years after 1897.[111] These campaigns were decisively advanced by the work of Wheatley in securing the support of Glasgow's Roman hierarchy to the cause of Labour (and with it the mass of

Irish and Catholic votes), and in drafting a popular programme of local authority housing around the '£8 Cottage Scheme' in the pre-War period. The simple and effective principle of financing cheaper and more comfortable cottages from the surpluses accumulated in operating Glasgow's fine tram system, was perhaps the single most crucial contribution to the growth in support for Glasgow Labour and its housing proposals.[112] Yet it required the organising ability of Andrew McBride to launch the Labour Party's Housing Committee in 1913, committed to the implementation of the Cottage Scheme. The L.P.H.C. claimed to represent every labour organisation in Glasgow, emerging at a time of impending crisis described by McBride:[113]

They recognised that as private speculators had practically ceased building, and that as many houses were admitted to be unfit for human habitation, we felt we were in easy reach of a famine in housing.

At the same time the I.L.P. leadership did not ignore the political relevance of the rents and rates issue during 1913-14, with Wheatley writing in early 1914 of the 'desperate struggle for existence' against a powerful minority of houseowners.[114] After insistent agitation at the Corporation Chambers by Labour councillors, the municipality finally agreed to a rents investigation which found a substantial amount of overcharging from the 2,000 complaints examined. The bulk of the overcharging occurred in the Fairfield ward of Govan, where correct levies had been made in only 16 of almost 500 cases.[115] This demonstrated to many activists the likely consequences of housing shortages throughout Glasgow on the scale already recorded at Govan. It was in Govan also that prominent engineering tradesmen (of the A.S.E.) and active I.L.P. organisers were to be found recruiting at this time, Harry Hopkins wielding influence through the Govan Trades Council and John S. Taylor so involved in politics that he was denied Chairmanship of the A.S.E. branch in 1915 on the grounds that 'he had not been working at the trade for the past twelve months'.[116] At a political level, these multifarious initiatives were coordinated under the burgh Labour Representation Committees which promoted local councillors and offered a general organising link between the areas of Labour commitment. The Secretary of the

Govan L.R.C., George Galloway, took a particular interest in the housing and rents question not only in his own territory but across the Clyde at Partick.[117]

Yet it was not at City Chambers or Municipal council meetings that the struggle for the advance of working class issues under Labour began on Clydeside or elsewhere. Initiatives were made at a much lower and more immediate level in the fabric of local government, engaging agencies of various kinds and involving the transformation of established institutions which now began to function in a different way under local Labour leadership. The crucial first link in this bid for control of local government was the 'colonisation' of Glasgow's ward committees. These bodies were described in 1912, as associated with no political organisation but representing the wants and aspirations of the locality in the elections to the Town Council.[118] They occupied a peculiar significance in the Scottish and Glasgow contexts, given the persistence of local burgh government and the growing emphasis on the provision of social services. During the 1880s, a Parliamentary Bill had attempted to define their precise role and status, though its failure allowed them to continue as highly fluid and specific expressions of local popular politics.[119] This did not preclude a noticeable growth in their influence during the decades before the War, with Glasgow Corporation sending each committee copies of Corporation minutes and even providing facilities for their meetings at local municipal buildings.[120] Councillors were not formally accountable to such ward organisations, but in the overwhelmingly proletarian city of Glasgow they could not afford to ignore the aspirations of working class activists if they were to gain re-election. This helps to explain the remarkable advance in municipal services after the 1880s, for as the memorandum of 1912 noted, it was 'upon social questions that the election of Town Councillors in Glasgow turns'.[121]

For the rising generation of I.L.P. leaders, the advantages of these fluid and potentially powerful bodies was clear. They could undertake the administration of distress funds and the administration of unemployed applicants, thereby giving Labour people important experience in the autonomous running of public relief.[122] More specifically, ward committees provided the mechanism for the promotion of particular councillors in the local areas. There was also scope for the contributions of trade unionists and trades councillors to the wider debate on local conditions. Education and housing provision were of key importance in such burghs as Govan, where Harry Hopkins served as Govan Committeeman in the decade before the War. In 1904 he had persuaded his ward committee to contact Govan's Surveyor over back court deterioration, dangerous to children playing near sunken cellars.[123] When serving as Vice-Chairman later, Hopkins promoted the election of activists such as George Galloway (of the Labour Representation Committee), to the Govan School Board where contentious issues could be raised.[124] In 1909 the Govan Ward Committee made a serious effort to gain election — their success paving the way for closer contacts with the I.L.P. — followed by the request by Govan Trades Council (again with Hopkins involved) that free books and stationery should be distributed to 'all children attending the non-fee-paying State-aided schools'.[125] During the same decade, Govan's committee protested at the influence and bias of the *Govan Press* in its handling of local issues.[126]

Taking much of their support from tenants' organisations and local industrial workers, ward committees were engaged in wider struggles on the issues of housing and rents on Clydeside. This became a more pronounced feature of their discussions after 1914, when shortages were unprecedented at areas like Govan. One councillor who argued for a reduction of property taxes in 1917 received a hostile hearing, and upon the housing question generally the committee members 'were strong on the failure of private enterprise to cope with the question'.[127] Baillie Whitehead and Patrick Dollan received a better response when they warned of the massive reconstruction programme required, and Dollan reiterated Labour's position that reforms were obstructed at Glasgow because 'too many in the Council held property'.[128] It was a complaint that I.L.P. councillors took to City Chambers in increasing numbers at this period, openly challenging the alliance of propertied, financial and professional interests which continued to dominate local government under an ideology of gradualist improvements. One indication of the changes in attitudes and aspirations that were sweeping the ward committees themselves at this time, is the belated review of ward rolls and admission of women to franchise and membership of the committees.[129]

In our existing accounts of working class struggle on Clydeside, we have a much fuller account of the revolutionary socialist parties than the growth of mass support for the I.L.P. and Labour Party policies. This is a serious overstatement of their scale and significance in the first two decades of the century, when they struggled against dogmatism, rivalry and endemic factionalism in their attempts to create a popular programme — and on many occasions failed to recognise the disastrous implications of sectarian politics. The Socialist Labour Party has been accorded a crucial role in the leadership of class struggles by writers such as Hinton and Challinor, whose works remain an authoritative interpretation of these years.[130] Their focus of attention, like that of the S.L.P. itself, remains overwhelmingly industrial and their understanding of political expression restricted to an exploration of workplace initiatives and the politicised leadership provided by a handful of trained cadres.

It is illuminating to chart the evolution of the S.L.P. and other revolutionary groups in the pre-War years as a contrast to the development of the Labour Party (which was itself only formed on a Glasgow-wide basis after various negotiations between distinct elements in 1910). The Socialist Labour Party was moulded from the Scottish branches of the Marxist-inspired Social Democratic Federation which split away from Hyndman's leadership in 1903.[131] This had been provoked by the attacks on both Hyndman and Quelch by the Scottish activist Yates, himself heavily influenced by the syndicalist teachings of Daniel De Leon in the United States. Their quest for purity of doctrine and rejection of political or industrial pragmatism was dramatically displayed when they expelled their own Secretary — Neil Maclean — for participating in the unemployment protests of 1908.[132] Anything which detracted from the revolutionary role of industrial unionism and distracted workers from their destiny at the workplace was bitterly criticised. Their most notable success was in collaboration with the Advocates of Industrial Unionism (an offshoot of the 'Wobblies'), in opposing management policies at the Clydebank factory of American-owned Singers. The subsequent smashing of the union after a strike in 1911, is portrayed as a salutary event by Hinton who suggests that the dispersal of S.L.P. cadres throughout Clydeside created a situation whereby the Party became 'the major political influence of the shop stewards' movement'.[133] Given its influence over key individuals such as MacManus, Muir and Clark, the S.L.P. made an unquestionable contribution to the growing effectiveness of

Clyde shop stewards, but its impact on local politics and social issues was understandably marginal. Even at the workplace, its impact on coordinating committees in engineering and munitions plants should not be exaggerated to the exclusion of I.L.P. and S.D.F. activists like Messer, Kirkwood, Gallacher and Hopkins.

After the departure of the syndicalist contingent, the remnants of the Social Democratic Federation were organised in Scotland by the young John Maclean and his lieutenant James MacDougall.[134] Maclean was a bitter critic of the 'opportunism' of the I.L.P. and Labour Party, as well as those departing for the syndicalist cause. On the formation of an official City Labour Party at Glasgow in 1910, Maclean accused the Labour Party of serving the needs of Liberalism at national and local levels.[135] Then he joined with some local I.L.P.ers to found the Social Democratic Party, and the next year established the British Socialist Party as the authentic heirs to the teachings of Marx and Engels.[136] Like the S.L.P., actual membership of the B.S.P. was miniscule before the War and though the S.D.F. had fought municipal elections from the 1890s, they were not serious rivals to the Labour Party at industrial or political elections. The greatest contribution of Maclean and the B.S.P. was the theoretical clarity and cogent criticism which they brought to a range of contemporary debates. Foreshadowing his later successes as an accessible teacher of Marxist economics, Maclean wrote extensively in local newspapers (as well as establishing *Vanguard* for the B.S.P.), on capitalist production and using immediate policies as examples of class struggle. In 1904 he argued strongly against speculative building of working class housing, whilst dismissing the idea that municipal services represented a socialist form of consumption. Maclean wrote of one apologist for public utilities:[137]

. . . what he really means is municipal capitalism. . . . We socialists support municipal capitalism because it is the line of least resistance to socialist society.

Yet Maclean was unable to develop a platform of practical reforms which rivalled those of Wheatley and Dollan in the Labour ranks, nor did his writings and pamphlets resolve the continuing confusion and divisions over innovation and change at the workplace. Local engineering workers, for example, were stubborn in their defence of craft practices but uncertain on responses to mechanisation or non-skilled recruitment. Muir and Kirkwood had enough experience of Weir and Beardmore respectively to recognise the practical obstacles to coherence in their resistance. Unlike housing and unemployment relief, there was a distinct absence of practical policies on industrial reform which Maclean could do little to resolve.

CHAPTER FIVE

The origins of the Wartime crisis: housing conditions and industrial unrest

Older accounts of 'Red Clydeside' included in the autobiographies of outstanding activists, such as that of William Gallacher, presented the Glasgow rent strike as an important chapter in the rise of a unified class struggle which culminated in the founding of the Clyde Workers' Committee and the fight against dilution.[138] More recent interpretations acknowledge the significance of this campaign, but suggest its fundamental isolation from the initiatives of the shop stewards and even the 'failure' of munitions workers to seize upon the rent strike to consolidate their opposition to an oppressive state machine.[139] In each case it is assumed that industrial employers and government officials had a systematic strategy of labour subordination, which complemented the general mobilisation of propertied interests to increase profits and accumulation during the War. Crucial in the failure of the working class to secure a decisive shift in economic and social power at this time, it is argued, were the divisions which appeared amongst the shop stewards and the hesitation over particular objectives in industry and local or national politics.

These explanations of Wartime conflicts suffer from both a narrowing of attention to workplace developments and a certain misunderstanding of state intervention. For the transition from a peacetime laissez faire economy to what became government regulation of production for a total war, involved a fundamental shift within the State which was only accomplished after a series of economic and political crises. Thus the essential character of state control and its relationship to different elements of the propertied interests underwent a radical transformation which cannot be encompassed within the notion of a 'servile state', comprising bourgeois institutions dressed for war. We also need to recognise the potential for antagonism within the ranks of capital and labour alike at this period, rather than assuming that areas of class conflict stimulate a spontaneous mobilisation of propertied and proletariat. High rents and tenant unrest did not immediately bring industrialists into action behind landlords or state repression of rent strikes, any more than munitions or dilution struggles fused shipyard and engineering trades (still less textiles, building or casual workers) in opposition to management. The experiences of the pre-War years had demonstrated that alliances between sections of the working class and their representatives had to be patiently constructed, often against the powerful currents of reaction and conservatism. If the Roman Catholic Church had been pacified by the Labour Party before 1914, there were still signs of resurgent Orangeism and Masonry around the debates on Home Rule and social reform at Glasgow and elsewhere. Even similar alignments of workers and tenants took the determined work of activists such as Hopkins in Govan and Neil Maclean in Partick to bring to fruition, whilst socialist parties themselves remained infected with dogmatism and sectarianism on the eve of War.

The extent to which organisations at work, among tenants and women, and in politics gathered local support depended to a considerable degree on their ability to elaborate and develop the existing customs and practices of working people. Many of the most successful tenant associations, for example, were sponsored or led by the Labour Party activists but remained autonomous organisations with a non-political ruling on access and participation. They also developed committees and meetings which facilitated the attendance of housewives, industrial workers and shopkeepers rather than professional politicians. Accountability to local workers was as much a feature of feminist and tenant associations as it was of shop stewards' committees and Labour delegations for election to the city authorities. Alongside the growth of fresh organisations came the colonisation and capture of traditional institutions, particularly the ward committees in Scottish burghs. Their functions were redirected under the talented leadership of residents supported by I.L.P. branches. As the organisation and strength of the Labour Party increased, so did its representation on School Boards, Corporation committees and agencies responsible for the distribution of public relief.

Although this wave of increased participation was itself

a reaction against the existing hierarchy of authority in society and politics, it did not resolve the problem of accountability within working class organisations. There were clear differences not only between 'rank and file' shop stewards and their union officials, but between Labour councillors or tenant leaders and their constituents. It is possible to trace a mounting challenge to capitalist authority in legal contests over housing as much as in unionisation of manual and non-manual workers, but numerous forms of authority were themselves autonomous of direct capitalist control and therefore not completely dependent on propertied rights for their maintenance. Thus the struggles against male domination of the franchise and workplace, or the challenges to union leadership and Parliamentary Labour policies, involved their own problems and contradictions within the context of continuing capitalist production. This complicated relationship between working class demands and specific conditions of struggle, makes generalisation about 'rank and file' aspirations and the objective implications of particular campaigns difficult. It is within the changing situation of class relations that we must interpret the distinct campaigns of these years, taking into account not only conflicts between but also within class interests and their consequences for political advance. This plurality of immediate interests and loyalties within classes was, on occasion, as much a dynamic of change as more explicitly 'class' conflicts.

There were also very clear limitations to the influence and hegemony of these organisations within the working class. Ideological as well as sectional divisions continued to exist, not least between strong loyalism amongst Protestant shipyard workers and the Catholic nationalism of Irish immigrants. Wheatley's contribution was to reject each persuasion as the basis for mobilisation around the Labour Party. Nor did the Labour pioneers avoid the issue of leadership and of enlisting the support of those unwilling to accept recruitment to the party organisation. Housing campaigns involved staid Liberal or Unionist supporters as well as men and women committed to socialism, differing in their aspirations but sharing broader concepts of 'justice' and 'fairness' that were to become crucial in the public rhetoric of the rents campaigns. Perhaps the most important weakness of the I.L.P. and Labour Party programmes was the limited scope they gave for discussion of workplace conflict and control. Relying upon the active support of craft and labour unions in local wards and burghs as well as national politics, the Labour Party focused on problems of wage levels and working conditions for municipal employees without extending the debate to expanding industries (such as engineering and ship-building) from which they drew their support. This left much of the initiative to an S.L.P. lacking Labour's (or even the B.S.P.'s) wider perspective on social conditions and constitutional politics. It also made for a sharper distinction of struggles that held potential for practical collaboration. In examining the conflicts of 1915-16, it is important to identify this distance between campaigns as well as emphasising the vital areas of contact in the separate movements and their leadership.

CHAPTER SIX

Spreading discontents: workplace conflict and state control, 1914-15

There were signs of serious unrest in Clydeside's heavy industries well before the outbreak of War swept thousands of journeymen into the forces and brought thousands more into the munitions sectors of the Clyde valley. The region dominated the Scottish shipbuilding and marine engineering industries, whilst manufacturing half of all the boilers built in the U.K. at this period. The metal industries as a whole employed almost 30% of the working population and were immediately escalated to national strategic importance as government departments multiplied their orders for vital war materials.[140] The question was no longer that of international competition and profit margins but of industrial and political survival as the largest military imperialist power. This situation only gradually dawned upon capitalists and politicians who also expected the War to last a few months, rather than consuming over four years' of production and millions of men. It was in this period of division and uncertainties that the early industrial confrontations occurred, becoming themselves part of a protracted transition to the wartime state.

In June 1914 the engineering employers were presented with a collective demand for a 48 hour week from 32 unions on Clydeside, which provoked some division of business opinion.[141] The next month the Clyde District Committee of the engineering union, A.S.E., gave formal notice of a claim for 2d. an hour increase in journeymen's wages.[142] On the outbreak of hostilities in Europe, the employers insisted on the preservation of the peacetime status quo until the resolution of the crisis, though they had anticipated conflicts for some time.[143] In January 1915 the District Committee responded to a further rejection of their wage claim by an emphatic protest, though the local officials — Bunton and Brody — wrote and telephoned the masters' association to assure them that 'the letter of the Glasgow District Secretary should be treated as an unofficial communication'.[144] There arose a clear division between the aggressive initiatives of the engineering Committee members, and the clandestine actions of moderate officials seeking to avoid confrontation at almost any price.[145] This letter of the District Committee had in fact notified the employers of an intention to strike from January 20th in the absence of a general increase of 2d. per hour.

At this point the A.S.E. were only in the forefront of a handful of engineering unions (including the machinists), who were demanding the increase and their reasoning was based upon a widespread recognition of rises in living costs as much as anomalies between Clydeside and other districts. It is interesting that at this early stage, the unpopular actions of William Weir in seeking to attract foreign labour to Britain with higher wages than trade rates were only one element in a general attack on profiteering amongst Clydeside employers. As the official delegations to the employers put it:[146]

Increased cost of living — food, clothes and rent — justifies advance. . . . Employers are making a rich harvest and margin rates on Government contracts and men should get a share. . . . The feeling of the men is very strong that they should be better remunerated for their labour, and if settlement not arrived at Society Officials may have difficulty in keeping them at work.

The industrialists responded to this determined front from even society officials, by suggesting that their employees should be grateful for the opportunity to work unlimited overtime *and* to participate in the piecework and premium bonus schemes in industry, which 'more than covered the increased cost of living'. After some of the unions had put the masters' offer of ½d. per hour increase, the A.S.E. proceeded to an overtime ban (despite the arguments of Bunton) in late-January 1915.[147] Here again such unions as the Coppersmiths were as militant as the A.S.E. and other societies, and it was in an attempt to stem a rising tide of unrest that the employers conceded an advance of ¾d. per hour — to last for the duration of the War.[148] Before the unions had sufficient time to digest this initiative of 10th February, they were overtaken by the extraordinary provocation of William Weir, whose importation of American workmen and unbridled attacks on Clyde journeymen precipitated a fresh crisis.[149] This brought engineers out not only at Cathcart but in marine engineering works along the river in which essential Admiralty work was being completed.

Such a show of unqualified aggression from the employers, supported by shipbuilding firms, opened up an area of strong disagreement between industrialists and the state. The Admiralty, in particular, were dubious about the wisdom of refusing further advances once the Weir troubles arose and Richmond (Weir's managing director) rejected major concessions to the men.[150] In this situation the Engineering Federation at London sent Allan Smith to interview Admiralty ministers and *he* insisted on the attendance of the Executive Council of the A.S.E., whilst back on Clydeside Bunton was informing the employers privately that he 'entirely disapproved' of his members' actions and had instructed them to return to work.[151] By 20th February the Clyde employers were suspicious of concessions that might be negotiated over their heads at London, particularly after Admiralty representatives suggested that 'in national interests . . . it looked as if whatever concession was necessary to secure a resumption of work would have to be made'.[152] This impression was confirmed by the decision of the Clyde Brassmoulders (Gallacher's union) to join the strike movement from the 22nd, though this was narrowly averted by society officials, whilst on the 18th Gallacher had joined with I.L.P.ers, Clark, Kirkwood and Messer to form the Central Labour Withholding Committee.[153] Government officials were particularly concerned at the spectacle of a 'revolt of the men against their own Executive', whereas the employers appeared assured by the dilemma of local society officials on the continuance of the strikes that had spread across Clydeside.[154] Engineering employers were represented at London by the most ruthless of managerialist firms, with Henderson, Richmond and Rowan Thomson in the capital by 22nd February.[155] Their strategy was to impress upon the government departments the futility and even danger of such major concessions as a 2d. increase,arguing that they felt:[156]

. . .very strongly the desirability of having the full effects of such a course upon the industrial situation placed before the authorities.

Matters were clearly coming to a head when the Brassmoulders did come out in support of the strike movement on 26th February, the same day that the government Committee on Production made an offer of arbitration — supported by the A.S.E. national executive.[157] Within a few days Isaac Mitchell arrived to resolve the Brassmoulders' own strike, as Johnstone and Renfrew engineering workers drifted back to work ahead of their Glasgow counterparts.[158] The engineering workers tacitly accepted the C.O.P.'s award of a 1d. hour increase in late-March 1915, though the Brassmoulders continued their struggle beyond this (possibly swayed by the articulate leadership of local shop stewards such as Gallacher), until their case was also settled by early April.[159]

The unexpected support attracted by the strike waves of February 1915, had significant implications for the relations between state and employers as well as between different sections of the workforce. Government ministers and officials were convinced that the Defence of the Realm Acts were inadequate to prevent the disruption of production and threats to the War effort. Industrialists were equally critical of existing regulations but attempted to use the February crisis to force the Government's arm on coercive repression of strikers, apparently envisaging some style of industrial conscription to keep the men at work. On their side, the trade unions were still primarily concerned with securing wage increases to offset rising living costs, though clear antagonisms were evident within district committees between officials and shop delegates as well as a degree of disagreement between local officials and national executive on certain issues. The genesis of the Labour Withholding Committee on Clydeside should not obscure the work of shop stewards' and shipyard vigilance committees, though it marked a useful advance in coordination between unions at an unofficial level. Yet it is clear that engineering workers (and more particularly skilled fitters and turners), were only one element in the spreading discontents of 1914-15, even if they were prominent in moves of many unions to secure 48 hours and substantial wage increases. Perhaps the more serious consequence of the February strikes for the Government, rather than the financial burdens of wages rises upon War contracts, was the sustained challenge to the authority of management and even union direction in industry. Only by proposing conciliation procedures were the Admiralty and other departments able to recapture the support of striking engineering and shipyard trades.

Similar difficulties and divisions appeared when the Government attempted to alleviate this situation by introducing legislation to establish the Ministry of Munitions (under Lloyd George), and introduce fresh provisions to avert and penalise industrial disputes. Despite its later controversial history, this Munitions legislation was more the creation of trade union leaders and civil servants than of industrial employers or businessmen. Only if we telescope the developments of late 1915-16 into the early months of 1915, ignoring contemporary responses by industrialists, can we portray Munitions legislation and the dilution campaigns as the offspring of a businessman's government and a 'servile state'. In June 1915, the Clydeside engineering association wrote of their 'disappointed feeling' that the national federation had given no lead on wages policies, 'or anything else in the present crucial times'. They went on to record bitterly, that they:[160]

considered it extraordinary that the federation should be inarticulate when important labour legislation was being promoted by the Minister of Munitions.

Allan Smith was forced to reply that munitions employers were seriously out of favour with the Government, due to their repeated failures to meet delivery dates on production levels promised. Lloyd George hoped to outflank the opposition of industrialists as well as meet the challenge of industrial militants by reaching an accommodation with national executives of unions and attracting more enlightened employers to the Munitions Ministry (including the social investigator Rowntree). Further progress was hoped from the regional Armaments Committees set up in areas such as west Scotland during 1915, which offered a forum for discussion between employers and trade unionists on the problems of increasing output.[161]

Unfortunately for the optimists, the Munitions legislation also placed severe limitations on the free movement of labour at a period of unprecedented labour shortages by introducing a system of Clearance Lines for munition workers. It was pointed out in Parliament by one Liberal M.P. for Glasgow, that this placed the workman in the unique position of being 'the only man who cannot sell the commodity he has, namely his labour in the open market'.[162] Even without the bitter memories of Discharge Notes in shipbuilding and engineering, this restriction almost inevitably gave rise to friction in administration — which was immeasurably worsened by the repressive use immediately made of the Act by ruthless shipbuilding management. Already in June 1915, one of the Parkhead Forge shop stewards and colleague of Kirkwood had been prosecuted for assault on another workman and only freed from gaol after A.S.E. official efforts.[163] It was in August 1915 that the first major crisis swept Clydeside over the Munitions legislation when Fairfields refused a clean Clearance Certification to two shipwrights dismissed for 'slacking' at the shipyard. On the outbreak of a strike amongst the Govan shipwrights, the Munitions Ministry sanctioned the prosecution of the men — under the Defence of the Realm Act before a Munitions Tribunal in early September.[164] Seventeen shipwrights were fined £10 each for leaving their work but in refusing to pay these penalities asked Harry Hopkins (President of the Govan Trades Council though an A.S.E. member), to explain their sense of grievance at 'the wrong of a money penalty out of all proportion to the offence'. Hopkins warned Lloyd George that such unfair treatment of these shipwrights would excite the strongest sympathy among 'all classes of Trade Unionists and workers, and its ultimate effect will be disastrous'.[165] Faced with the firm refusal of the Minister to interfere with these industrial courts, or to qualify the quasi-judicial regulation of workplace customs, Hopkins launched a general appeal for union resistance to the Munitions Act and a campaign for its repeal.[166] When the shipwrights were imprisoned for refusing to pay the fines and deserted by their own society officials, Hopkins and the Govan Trades Council seized the initiative by telegraphing Lloyd George on 13th October that unless the men were released within three days their fellow shipwrights would again strike.[167] As the Govan trade unionists prepared to bring out thousands of men on the issue of the Munitions legislation and in support of gaoled workers, the Government despatched Isaac Mitchell north to report on the deteriorating situation. At this point Lloyd George's lieutenant and confidante, Addison, noted that despatches reaching London varied from descriptions of reasonable tranquillity to reports that 'there was certain to be a revolutionary outbreak tomorrow', hence the fact-finding mission of Mitchell.[168] Then on 15th October, the Cabinet appointed a special enquiry into the Clyde troubles under Lord Balfour and Lynden Macassey, which conducted some of its hearings at the gaol where the shipwrights were incarcerated — but concluding their proceedings on 21st October without the release of the men.[169] Tension continued to mount and, in the words of a moderate official of the Boilermakers' Society, the 'Clyde at the present time was like a volcano ready to burst'.[170] Anger and frustration spread throughout the Shipwrights' Society itself and on 23rd October its official leadership demanded the release of the men, pending further industrial action within three days if no satisfactory progress was made.[171] The Govan Trades Council was preparing for a widespread series of strikes when Lloyd George skilfully persuaded the Society officials to pay the fines on the 27th October, thereby defusing a dangerous situation on Clydeside for employers and state alike.[172]

The struggles over the implementation of the Munitions Act assumed such momentum in the Autumn of 1915, not only because of the powerful resistance to state coercion from trade unionists. Engineering and shipbuilding employers were both watching the progress of dilution initiatives with some anxiety, even in the forms of labour dilution and simplification of working methods would be very different in each sector. In July and August of 1915, the progressive firm of Langs at Johnstone (beyond Paisley) faced craft resistance when attempting to introduce female dilutees at their lathe-making works.[173] The following month, engineering firms at Glasgow heard that widespread protests had greeted the use of unrecognised workers on naval drilling work at Barrow and Merseyside as well as the Clyde itself.[174] Such employers were understandably reluctant to instigate a concerted offensive on the dilution issue when the Munitions Act necessary to its implementation was itself under threat from the unions. Behind this expressed reservation lay other considerations: on the one hand the employers were determined to assert their managerial control over dilution in Wartime industry and extremely sceptical of the negotiating procedures involved in the regional Armaments Production Committees; on the other, managements were themselves uncertain as to the effectiveness of dilution arrangements (more particularly in the case of shipbuilding), and were eager to present the obstacles to change as simply that of union sabotage. There is little evidence that the Scottish industrialists made a serious attempt to support the Armaments Committees or to push through individual dilution agreements with their shop stewards. Thus in October 1915, the engineering employers' association wrote to the Ministry of Munitions, at the time of continuing Lang troubles and Fairfield conflict, that:[175]

If the employers were assured that the active support of the Ministry would be given in the event of trouble arising through the introduction of these changes, every endeavour would be made to secure such relaxations of restrictions as are permitted by the Act.

The hard-line managements now in the leadership of the masters' associations were especially criticial of the Circular L2 distributed by the Ministry in elaboration of the Act, which stipulated comparable wage levels for women undertaking jobs usually carried out by skilled workmen. For the employers, this removed all the pecuniary advantages of dilution and made them decidedly sceptical of the utility of drastic changes in their workforce.[176]

When the dilution officials Cramond and Paterson arrived to investigate the slow progress of dilution in both engineering and shipbuilding works during December 1915, therefore, they found a surprising lethargy amongst the major employers. As the proceedings of the meeting make clear, Paterson was openly critical of this lack in business initiatives:[177]

There had been no general dilution of skilled labour.

Employers made general statements only to the effect that their workmen will not allow the practical removal of restrictions. . . . He therefore suggested that firms should make a survey of all work being done, with a view to furnishing to the Ministry the extent to which dilution could be arranged, provided Trade Union restrictions were removed . . .

This was still very much the situation when Lloyd George himself arrived on Clydeside during the Christmas of 1915, expecting a hero's welcome but facing the unflinching hostility of shop stewards such as Kirkwood and the noisy reception in Glasgow at a public meeting attended by hundreds of workmen. To working people with memories of the 2d. hour dispute, Munitions Tribunal coercion, ineffectual enquiries into industry unrest, aggressive strategies from the employers — including Weir's importation of Canadian workmen and the Lang dilution threat, and the general deterioration in living costs and housing conditions, Lloyd George personified the arrogance of a remote government and its repressive legislation. It was to this open confrontation of Scotland's working class and the Wartime state that the rent strikes made such a powerful contribution.

CHAPTER SEVEN

Rent Strikes and working class organisation on Clydeside in 1915

Just as industrial conflicts were foreshadowed in the campaigns of early 1914, so there were clear signs of the coming unrest over rents in the pre-War tenant protests. Housing shortages were a major concern to working class families after 1911, even if they could afford the rents asked for large tenement flats, as the proportions of the housing stock standing unoccupied declined from one in ten or less in districts such as Clydebank, Govan and Partick to less than one in a hundred in many of the main shipbuilding burghs by 1914.[178] The continued expansion of industry amidst the contraction of construction placed serious strains on the houses available, driving up rents and reducing the incentives to carry out repairs and improvements. According to official experts of Glasgow's city administration, the Corporation had required as many as 65,000 new houses over the three years from 1912, whereas only 1,400 were in fact built.[179] The bitter complaints at unjustified and unlawful exactions which were widespread in the Fairfield ward of Govan during 1914, as well as the noticeable trend towards legal and direct resistance to ejectment notices at Glasgow, both testify to the intensification of landlord-tenant conflict before the coming of War. It also seems likely that the introduction of even limited social legislation during the age of Liberal welfare reform, had an adverse affect on property and housing investment even if they hardly touched real propertied interests.[180]

The outbreak of War and sudden immigration of thousands of workers, with almost equal numbers of local men leaving to join the expeditionary forces and naval fleets beyond Scotland, had a dramatic impact upon Clydeside housing. Most severely affected were the already hard-pressed burghs nearest Glasgow, such as Partick and Govan, which had virtually no accommodation left by early 1915.[181] Nearby districts such as Ibrox and Whiteinch were feeling the effects by 1915, whilst the east side of the city (particularly the Shettleston neighbourhoods which housed

Parkhead Forge employees), was almost as badly hit.[182] Perhaps worst-placed of all were those outlying burghs of Clydebank and Dalmuir, Greenock and Port Glasgow, which were incapable of absorbing the surplus population which full production demanded. Any district which possessed a large engineering, shipbuilding or steel works — whether it was the Albion Motor Plant or North British Diesel works at Scotstoun or the great railway locomotive shops at Springburn — was facing an acute housing shortage by the early months of 1915. The belated attempts of Addison and the Munitions Ministry to protect naval armaments plants by extra government housing at Rosyth, Clydeside and Woolwich came too late with too little.[183]

Pressures on available housing were quickly translated into the direct intimidation of some groups of tenants finding difficulty coping with the rising costs of living. With reports of scarcity rents and the harassment of soldiers' wives and dependants carried in Labour's weekly paper *Forward* as early as August 1914.[184] The state's Emergency Powers Act protected such groups provided they could demonstrate that their predicament was caused by War conditions, which effectively rendered eviction impossible.[185] Those unable to appeal against ejectment warrants on these grounds were not accorded the same privileges, with Sheriffs granting warrants in November 1914 unimpeded by any claim of special consideration.[186] Despite the early intervention of the state on treatment of dependants whose wage-earners were now active servicemen, the harassment of the wives and children of soldiers as well as the alleged intimidation of aged tenants and pensioners continued to be publicised by I.L.P. papers and other activists throughout 1915. Such stories were often used as decisive proof of the inhumane profiteering of landlords and factors, and the physical defence of such tenants became an important focus for the rallying of support by resistance leaders.

An early contribution was secured from Trades Councils at Christmas 1914, when Willie Shaw of Glasgow and Harry Hopkins of Govan joined a deputation of women in the City Chambers to complain of housing conditions.[187] This followed an attempt by Hopkins to create a more formal connection between the Councils, as well as to support the campaign of Labour Party workers for a general debate on municipal building commitments.[188] Such initiatives were reinforced by the decision of the Glasgow Houseowners'

Association shortly afterwards, to attempt a guaranteed minimum of six per cent return on housing investment at Glasgow. As Andrew McBride told the large I.L.P. conference on housing in January 1915, the serious danger to the Glasgow landlords, was:[189]

not the Government, nor even the present Town Council; their real danger lies in the growing volume of public discontent which is evident among every class of tenant.

It was not the slum dwellers of Cowcaddens or Plantation that were raising their voice in protest, McBride and the Labour Party Housing Committee warned, but the better and more affluent groups of tenants who resented the advantage taken by a minority of property-owners. Then in February 1915, the Trades Council at Clydebank took up the leadership of the anti-landlord campaign by proposing an April demonstration to highlight the burgh's difficulties and protest against increased rents by passing 'a resolution in favour of establishing Fair Rents Courts'.[190] Within two months another trades council, this time in the hardest-pressed shipbuilding burgh of Greenock at the mouth of the Clyde, passed a resolution in favour of immediate action by the Government to prevent:[191]

property owners raising rents at this unprecedented time, such as the passing of a prohibition order or the establishment of a Fair Rent Court.

The Glasgow Trades Council responded by appointing their President, Shanks, to serve on the Clydebank Demonstration Committee and by endorsing the resolution proposed by its Greenock counterpart in April, though when Clydebank again took the lead by forming a Fair Rents League in May 1915, Glasgow members declined the invitation to participate.[192] This was despite the city's own January resolution calling on the Government to take whatever steps were needed to 'prevent the uncalled for increase in the cost of the necessaries of life', and reflects the continued influence of moderates in the Glasgow body despite the influence of Shinwell amongst others.[193]

During the Spring and Summer of 1915, it was very much left to the initiatives of the tenants themselves to offer resistance to the increases demanded by factors in areas such as Govan and Partick, even if the local Labour branches promised full support once any action was under way. In fact, it is likely that the Labour Party itself was more hopeful of petitions and representations of Glasgow Corporation and national government, coupled with traditional forms of legal obstruction, than the unfamiliar tactic of a concentrated rent strike against one or more factors. In February 1915, the Glasgow Women's Housing Association did organise the first of many meetings at the Morris Hall to protest against rent increases, chaired by Mary B. Laird and addressed by John S. Taylor and Patrick Dollan as well as Harry Hopkins.[194] This afternoon gathering was opened with songs and music as well as socialist readings, though there was as yet no mention of non-legal action from the women who the speakers were addressing.

Labour agitation against the owners continued in the political press with stories of evictions of servicemen's wives, such as one mother forced to leave her home after being too ill to attend a Court hearing to plead her own case. Patrick Dollan commented of this case that the furniture was deposited in the homes of neighbours, 'who, in my opinion, should not have allowed the eviction to take place'.[195] This theme of the 'unpatriotic' action of factors, and of tenants refusing to assist the plight of patriotic victims became a powerful aspect of Labour's popular journalism. In February 1915, Dollan was recorded as telling the Govan Tenants' Defence Association (founded by Wardley before the War), that the landlords 'were no better than the Huns. They were worse than spies'. He expressed his regret that the enlisted men had not settled with landlords in Govan and Glasgow before leaving for France, making deliberate use of the inflammatory recruiting sentiments to turn women and men against their factors.[186] Another early characteristic of the agitation amongst tenants was the tactical identification of the landlord and his rent increases as the crucial element in a general spiral of living costs which had begun after the outbreak of War. Rising prices in foodstuffs were causing dissatisfaction when the notices of intended rent increases arrived during the early months of 1915, identifiable as the 'stubborn facts within the daily experience of the workmen'.[197] I.L.P. activists with an intimate understanding of the customary resistance to even marginal increases in rents and the growing hostility to factors as the emissaries of fresh demands and deprivation, quickly appraised the depth of anti-landlord feeling in working class neighbourhoods.

Glasgow Women's Housing Association

(NON-PARTY ORGANISATION)

To Secure Municipal Housing Free of Interest.

UNDER THE ABOVE AUSPICES A

MEETING of WOMEN

WILL BE HELD IN THE

MORRIS HALL, 68 Shaw St.,

On TUESDAY, 16th FEB., at 3 p.m.,

To PROTEST against the INCREASE IN RENTS.

While at this moment all sections of the community, especially Women, are called upon to make sacrifices, the patriotic President of the Houseowners' Association, at their Annual Meeting, stated **"That this was the time to raise Rents,"** and **Rents are now being raised.**

Mrs. MARY BURNS LAIRD in the Chair.

COUNC. JOHN S. TAYLOR,
COUNC. P. J. DOLLAN,
HARRY HOPKINS.

WILL ADDRESS THE MEETING.

MUSICAL SELECTIONS, SONGS AND READINGS.

COLLECTION TO DEFRAY EXPENSES.

Pamphlet for meeting referred to opposite.

CHAPTER EIGHT

The Rent Strikes: Spring Offensive and Summer Campaigns

It was in Govan that the first signs of collective rent resistance appeared during the Spring of 1915, and it was the Govan wards that remained a stronghold of strike action during the succeeding months of struggle. There was a keen sense of unfair treatment at a municipal level on the rates question, since Govan had been promised immunity from rates increases for a number of years after the amalgamation with Glasgow in 1912, yet they had experienced rent advances on three or four occasions at times of general rises. Spokesmen such as Councillor John S. Taylor, argued that propertied interests were absorbing such increases without the justification of rates advances.[198] Then in April and May 1915, there came notices of further additions which provoked an immediate response from the experienced tenant groups. The local Women's Housing Association convened a public meeting under Mary L. Denny at the Cressy Hall on 21st May, addressed by prominent I.L.P.ers such as Alston, Dollan, McBride, Taylor and Wardley but with the resolutions all put and supported by local women themselves.[199] According to the Labour press, the Labour Representation Committee and the Party's Housing Committee were both prominent in the early organisation of the women's campaign.[200] Yet the same reports make clear that in several tenements the tenants had already decided to oppose their factors, and that after the public meetings were held it was 'the local tenants themselves' who canvassed support in the 250 houses affected by these increases, with 'the result that practically every man and woman signed the petition against the increases'.[201] Local mobilisation and direct personal contact laid the foundations for collective action in a way that a general appeal by Labour organisations could not have done.

It soon became clear that the focus of this first strike were the blocks of tenements in South Govan (or Linthouse), near the Stephens shipbuilding yard and a short distance from the Fairfield works. This substantial area of Govan consisted of good-quality tenements and stone cottages which were reputedly inhabited by draughtsmen, foremen and clerks as well as more affluent skilled workers.[202] It may well have been that these groups, who experienced a serious decline in real incomes as prices moved ahead of their staff salaries fixed at pre-War levels, participated in the growing protests at rent demands. David Wardley mobilised the Tenants' Association in defence of the strike and found that of 264 houses affected by the increases, 260 were committed to non-payment of the advances.[203] Direct action was sustained by collective responsibility, as the tenants became 'thoroughly organised' and appointed a secretary for each tenement, whilst fighting for the extension of the struggle to other properties and closes.[204] Rather than allowing the landlords to split the occupants by individual appeals and general threats, the tenants deliberately adopted the enforced collectivity of the tenement building and its lifestyle as the basis of their resistance. The fortified structure of traditional housing styles permitted an unusual degree of integration within the individual tenement, whilst making the forcible ejectment of the inhabitants extremely difficult without resort to substantial violence.

The initial response of the owners and factors was to threaten ejectment proceedings and Neilson (a powerful factoring firm with interests in Partick as well as Govan) among others, was accredited with responsibility for spreading rumours about the arrival of Harland and Wolff workers to take over the strikers' dwellings. Local women, led by Mrs Mary Barbour and Mrs Ferguson, contacted the shipbuilders directly and were assured by the managing director that Harlands had no such plans, and were even 'very pleased to hear that the tenants of the Govan district purpose refusing to pay these increased rents'.[205] Industrial employers were clearly unwilling to be drawn into a confrontation with working class families, whose male wage-earners worked at their Govan yards and engineering shops turning out vital munitions orders. The South Govan tenants also organised their own Tenants' Committee, and its secretary (Andrew Jeff) corresponded with the house-owners of the affected property in the area. These letters were published in the local press and Labour's papers, demonstrating to all concerned the intransigence of the propertied groups and their determination to extract from the occupants a better return on capital invested.[206] On behalf of the affected inhabitants, Labour councillors took up the arguments of the owner concerned and flatly contradicted the denial of previous war increases.[207] By June 1915, the deadlock was unbroken until the factors and their clients reluctantly agreed to withdraw the immediate notices of increase.[208]

The Summer months of 1915 witnessed a considerable escalation of the rents campaign, even though there were few sustained attempts to force through sizeable increases by the landlords. After the initial upsurge of tenant protest at South Govan, the movement accelerated only through the determined efforts of the Labour Party at Glasgow. Their contributions were made at three distinct levels: in the press and at public meetings, Labour leaders publicised the iniquities of the factors and called for retribution; in the local areas they encouraged and supported the autonomous activities of affected tenants, whom they often lived amongst; and in local government and Corporation they denounced the political influence of the propertied interests and called for a radical reappraisal in municipal housing programmes to meet the situation. As the momentum of the campaign grew, so other political activists and parties rose to public prominence, whilst the Labour leaders joined these elements in welcoming the support of industrial workers for the rents struggle, and in calling for intervention at a national level from the Wartime state.

The month of June saw the widespread publicisation of the housing question and the Labour's alternative strategy for dealing with continuing shortages. McBride's Labour Party Housing Committee organised a great demonstration of all the main working class groups to protest about recent rent rises, again listening to the acknowledged housing spokesmen such as Denny, Dollan, Taylor and Wheatley. The speakers made a direct comparison between the trade union struggles to maintain wages, and the responsibility of government to restrain Wartime increases — failing which the householders would themselves 'organise and refuse rents imposed' in an arbitrary way by the owners and factors.[209] At the same time there occurred a series of incidents in the east end of industrial Glasgow which brought John Wheatley's native district of Shettleston closer to the tenant movement. The most notorious case was that involving the McHugh family of William Street, who had a wounded father and two sons in the armed forces, when the housewife fell into arrears of less than £1 during Spring 1915. When the factor arrived to serve the ejectment warrant upon the mother and five children, a large crowd (variously estimated at between 500 and 4,000 people) gathered to defend the family. After nailing a Union Jack across the front door and listening to John Wheatley, the indignant neighbours went off in search of the factor at his offices and on arrival burned his effigy before the windows.[210] In this charged atmosphere, Glasgow's police force advised the civilian Sheriff's Officers (responsible for ejectment proceedings in civil law), against the execution of the warrant for fear of provoking a riot. The damage to the landlords' case had already been done, however, as Wheatley portrayed the episode as the latest in:[211]

a long line of cruel, crushing, insulting treatment to which the Capitalist class has subjected the working class.

Such distasteful examples of landlordism and its pursuit of profits from an 'economic' rent also helped the spread of resistance in the rest of Shettleston. Accommodation around the great Beardmore works at Parkhead was rapidly being filled when Govan and Partick were under stress in early 1915.[212] In the same month of June, the Richmond Park district of Glasgow found similar increases demanded by factors and at a public meeting the tenants decided to follow the Govan example, by fighting the rent-raisers and as in Govan a committee 'of two women for each close' was formed.[213] Once the battle was under way, a large demonstration was organised in support of the wider programme of Andrew McBride and the Labour Party Housing Committee.[214]

It was with this support growing in the streets of Glasgow that Labour councillors developed a case within the city Corporation for an official enquiry into rent increases. Wheatley argued in Council that the time had arrived when, 'steps should be taken to ensure that while a soldier was absent in defence of his country it would be illegal to turn his dependants out of their home', drawing upon his experience of the McHugh case to drive the point home.[215] Despite the vehement support of Labour councillors such as Izett and Taylor (both well known to the crowds at protest meetings), the Independents at City Chambers refused to swing the balance of support behind the resolution, which was lost by 46 votes to 34 after a stormy meeting. The local press still remained uncommitted where it was not actually interested in the struggle, though even the organ of the landowning interests acknowledged the gravity of the situation by the Summer of 1915.[216] The *Govan Press* suggested that the Cabinet itself was considering the possibility of establishing 'fair rent courts' in the munitions districts, since the earlier proposal of an official enquiry was no longer considered to be the best strategy to resolve the issue.[217]

Increasing official concern over the serious reports of rents unrest was reflected in the discussion of the matter in the region's Armaments Committee, made up of industrialists and trade unionists as well as civil servants.[218] But the first national airing of the housing problem came during the Parliamentary debates on the Munitions legislation passed in July. The Glasgow Liberal, Pringle, pointed out the iniquity of restricting the free sale of labour in the absence of similar regulations on prices and rents, suggesting that there should be 'tribunals of fixing rents'.[219] George Barnes of Gorbals, representing the Labour Party at Glasgow, was more emphatic in his denunciation of profiteering during Wartime but again demanded state intervention in the emergency situation. They met with little response from a Government enmeshed in the problems of raising massive public loans on the financial markets, and extremely wary of upsetting this delicate mechanism in the interests of scattered munitions workers. This wilful myopia was personified by Walter Long at the Local Government Board, who was perfectly happy to assist the coercion of trade unionists under the Munitions legislation but distinctly reluctant to undertake any restriction of rents or interest rates.[220] Lloyd George and Addison were heavily involved with the difficult implementation of the Act itself at this stage, and badly underestimated the significance of the housing and rents question.

While local and national government failed to grasp the nettle of Scottish unrest, trouble again descended on Govan during late July, This was caused by the transparent determination of Neilson and Sons, the powerful Govan and Partick factors, to break the rents resistance by selective increases at two tenements. The result was a united front by a majority of the tenants and a deputation of five women to interview the factor himself. Whereas Neilson argued that the high wages of the menfolk enabled them to pay higher rents, local housewives emphasised the case of soldiers' wives — but to little avail. After three weeks of stubborn resistance, one woman was persuaded that her neighbours were paying the rents and conceded the full amount, which led to general collapse of the strike.[221] In sight of victory, Neilson then tried to victimise the strike leaders by demanding further additions to cover the expense of previous non-payment. This provoked renewed struggles among a minority of tenants.[222] At the same time Neilsons consolidated their position by announcing similar increases across the Clyde at Partick, during August, though the inhabitants of one close immediately rallied against the demand. As in other districts of Glasgow, local tenants strongly attacked the 'exorbitant demands being made by the "patriotic" landlords . . . at this time of national crisis'.[223] Thereafter Partick was to become a storm centre of the rents struggle under the able leadership of I.L.P. journalist Andrew Hood and his *Partick Gazette*. With a solid background in the celebrated Kingston Branch of the I.L.P., Hood could call on the personal support of Dollan and Kerr among others while Neil Maclean's Partick Branch gave local assistance in the formation of the Partick Tenants' Committee.

Facing such organisation in both Govan and Partick, Neilson decided on the prosecution of two tenant leaders from the Stephen Drive section of South Govan. At the Sheriff Court both cases were brilliantly defended by the Labour advocate and Baillie, Rosslyn Mitchell. In one application he argued that the factor had accepted the old rent after notice of increase, thereby striking a bargain which provided no basis for prosecution. With Mrs Stewart he showed that the 'arrears' of 4s.6d. were demanded of the only tenant involved whose husband was on active service, and she was the 'only tenant who received notice of ejectment'. Counsel for the factors attempted to respond with a declaration of legitimate part-payment in the first case and of ignorance of circumstances in the latter, both of which were dismissed by the Sheriff.[224] Not a man to be beaten this easily, Neilson arranged that the acceptance of the old rent levels from his tenants should be received as 'payment on account', with the clear intention of further legal action at some future date.[225] The first court battle had gone to the tenants but it was only the start of the serious rent war.

During the remainder of September the Labour leadership consolidated its influence in Govan and Partick, whilst supporting the extension of the strike campaign to

Ibrox and Shettleston. In Ibrox there were rent increases averaging 2s.3d. per month for a room and kitchen, though the district was nominally exempted from rates increases until 1922. Patrick Dollan, Harry Hopkins and Andrew McBride were joined by John Maclean in speaking against any rent rises during the War, carried with the unanimous consent of 500 tenants at a public meeting.[226] Within a fortnight the protest in Ibrox had become so powerful that it surpassed Govan in numbers striking, helped by the visitations of a large tenants' committee upon householders who pledged themselves to refuse both increases and notices to quit.[227] On the same evening as the Ibrox public meeting, there occurred a similar gathering of tenants at Parkhead within the Shettleston area. The meeting was chaired by William Reid of Parkhead Forge, friend of Kirkwood and later I.L.P. tenant spokesman. There were vociferous attacks on the unpatriotic action of the factors raising rents, as well as bitter complaints about the gross inadequacy of Corporation building by speakers such as McBride.[228] This upsurge of protests in two districts distinguished by their religious affiliations and patronage of the two greatest Glasgow football clubs, indicates to some degree the extent of the challenge to existing authority relations and the erosion of sectarian divisions in the heat of the rent struggle. So prominent did the Shettleston campaign appear in late September, that one Glasgow newspaper assumed it marked the original area of resistance and went on to note, that:[229]

The revolt against the increase of house rents in Glasgow threatens to become a very big problem. . . . In view of the large number of munition workers who are interested in the agitation, it is possible that the Government may intervene.

This connection between munitions production and reasonable accommodation was to become much more explicit in the following weeks, though it is significant that by September there were Parkhead Forge workers directly affected by (and involved in) the rents question.

Govan and Partick's shipbuilding districts continued to capture the attention of employers and officials perturbed at the spreading support for rent strikes. An important development was seen when the Govan Ward Committee, encouraged by Hopkins and others, swung behind the local tenants' campaign.[230] At a time when the local shipwrights were being fined substantial sums for contravening labour regulations, this support of Hopkins for both tenant and industrial campaigns was to prove crucial. At Partick there were at least 140 tenants on strike by the end of the month, concentrated in thirteen closes with the majority described as 'of the respectable artisan type — skilled workers employed in the local shipyards and engineering shops'.[231] Their method of organisation was simple but extremely effective, whereby each of the occupants signed a 'round robin' letter refusing the increases. The same report also noted with some concern the participation of employees engaged in war munitions in the rents troubles, and the implications for industrial harmony. The backbone of this Partick strike was to be found amongst the 130 tenants factored by Neilson, though their ranks were swelled by the active campaigning of the Glasgow Women's Housing Association in open-air meetings where much 'strength and solidarity is given to the proceedings, and the feeling is ardent and deep'.[232] Like Ibrox and parts of Govan, Partick was well known for its strong Masonic and Orange Order contingents, though this did not prevent their adaptation of popular loyalist and patriotic slogans to attack the oppressive factors. One local woman who remained a life-long Tory and Orange Leader is reported to have played a prominent role in mobilising local tenants, borrowing a fishmonger's bell as the alarm against the approach of the enemy.[223]

These tactics appear to have been developed by the women themselves, through the experience of direct confrontation with figures who normally commanded respect and obedience. Humiliation of factors' clerks was the best antidote to the traditional intimidation by men wearing bowler hats and starched collars. Neilson countered the attempts to force the old rents upon him by simply refusing acceptance, upon which the housewives (after advice) decided to post the rents to his office. The factor then despatched his lieutenant to return these pre-War rent payments, laying the clerk open to the wrath of the women. The pelting of the deputy with flour and peasemeal forced him to retreat, whereupon he was 'chased from one of the streets by a number of women who upbraided him vociferously'.[234] Such incidents caused widespread comment and publicity in the Glasgow press, with few editors able to rescue the factors from satirical advice.[235] The general realisation of strategic position came only gradually even to the Labour activists, as the leadership sought to learn and apply the experiences of industrial conflict to the separate sphere of rents resistance. Councillor Alston pointed out at a public meeting at this time, that:[236]

They, who were protesting, must remember that their position was different from what it would be in an ordinary strike. In the usual strike the strikers could be locked out; in the present strike they were inside the houses, and could lock out the factor.

This principle of physical occupation could be asserted in action against the legalistic claim that possession represented an impregnable right in law. The conflict also placed the women in the forefront of the struggle against the agents of property, with even Labour journalists acknowledging the practical reliance of the whole campaign on housewives showing 'the rebel spirit'.[237] Evening meetings of the workmen held on the street corners of working class neighbourhoods sustained the movement, but it was in the working hours that the confrontation with factors usually took place.[238]

It was also in the late Summer of 1915, that other campaigns and organisations began to make a serious contribution to the rent strikes. Steadily gaining ground was the pacifist and anti-War crusade of the British Socialist Party allied with important sections of the I.L.P.. Mrs Helen Crawfurd joined with a variety of political speakers and conscientious objectors (including many clergymen), in her rallies against the War and the foundation of the Women's Peace Crusade in Scotland.[239] Equally energetic in the cause of peace was John Maclean, who participated in the Free Speech Committee at Glasgow and spoke at its first meeting — attracting 5,000 people — in September 1915, along with Hopkins, McColl, MacDougall and MacManus.[240] Yet the most telling arguments against the landlords were still coming from the tenants themselves, and the local councillors at strife-torn localities in Govan and Partick. Before the end of September, David Wardley and D. S. Denny of Govan led a deputation of aggrieved tenants to the City Chambers, where they presented resolutions passed at public meetings in Govan, Ibrox, Partick and Parkhead. Although the city councillors had also received numerous letters from ward committees at Ibrox, Cowlairs (Springburn) and Townhead, the Corporation rejected Wardley's proposal that the Government should take immediate action to prevent rent increases and also the suggestion of Rosslyn Mitchell that the council give immediate consideration to the tenant issue.[241] Clearly, if any progress was to be made on the housing question it would not begin at the City Chambers.

CHAPTER NINE

The Rent Strikes: Autumn Crisis

The Autumn of 1915 saw the rent unrest move from being a series of localised disturbances, even in the Clydeside context, to representing a national struggle capable of threatening Wartime production throughout Britain. The reasons for the extraordinary success of the rents campaign in attracting support and ultimately compelling the Government to take drastic action on rent rises, seem to be both obvious and complex. There certainly were sizeable increases in very specific areas of Clydeside during 1915, as well as a chronic housing shortage in localities vital to munitions production. Particular factors and owners took advantage of the scarcities to exact monopoly rents, sometimes even harassing the dependants of servicemen or War victims. Yet there is little evidence of a general and sustained pattern of rent rises even in the Summer of 1915, as is shown by the violent response of tenant groups to even limited rises by Neilson at Govan and Partick. Much of the discontent can be traced to the crude tactics and complete mistiming of their initiatives by the landlords, though the effectiveness of working class retaliation must be largely explained by the popularity of Labour leadership and the ability of different political and social organisations to mobilise in defence of the rent strikers. At the end of September, platform speakers were still concentrating on an official enquiry and to a lesser degree on fair rents tribunals, though the success of direct action gave the campaign a strong defensive position in the face of threats of further legal action against rent strikers. It was the growing threat of industrial action in support of the movement, not only in shipyards but from engineering plants as well, that made such a decisive impact on official calculations of costs and benefits during October and November of 1915.

There were reports of industrial troubles in many of the areas now being affected by rents unrest, with Cathcart, Dennistoun and Springburn possessing large engineering works as well as tenant campaigns in early October. [242] On 2nd October there took place a meeting of politicised shop stewards under Kirkwood on the dilution and other issues, and the following day the Clyde Trades Vigilance Committee was born.[243] The same evening that the C.T.V.C. was launched, Kirkwood sat down at his Shettleston home to draft a letter to Glasgow Corporation, possibly with the help of Wheatley. Writing on behalf of the men at Parkhead's 'Howitzer Shop', Kirkwood warned the councillors that they would regard any evictions as:[244]

an attack on the working class, which called for the most vigorous and extreme reply, and one which might have the most disastrous consequences. . . . If the nation is to have an adequate supply of the munitions of war, the workers must have adequate healthy housing accommodation.

This theme was taken up in the first of the large demonstrations or 'processions' to the City Chambers which took place on 7th October. There were over a thousand women drawn from at least six parts of the city, who appeared to observers as the well-dressed 'women and children of the respectable working class' impressing the public by their orderly progress and demeanour. Under banners proclaiming against the unpatriotic owners and stating that the 'Government Must Protect Our Homes from Germans and Landlords or the People Will Protect Themselves', the women sent a deputation under William Reid of Parkhead and David Denny of Govan to address the councillors.[245] Although the reports of the exchange vary in the press, it seems that Reid put his case moderately but firmly, telling the city authorities, that:[246]

the temper of the men was such that, in the event of wholesale evictions taking place . . . they would not hesitate not only to prevent evictions but to influence . . . Parliament by every other means in their power.

The Parkhead shop steward spelled out the disastrous consequences of industrial strikes in the engineering and shipbuilding trades, which the men were prepared to countenance if factors continued to assail the dependants of men at the front. The Corporation showed little reaction to either the deputation or the Kirkwood letter, though they did agree to a later debate on the whole subject of rent rises.

On the same day, 11th October, that Isaac Mitchell was sent north to investigate the continuing confrontations over the Munitions Act and shipwrights' prosecution, the

Secretary for Scotland (McKinnon Wood) came to Glasgow to enquire into rents unrest. On meeting the Labour councillors McBride and Stewart, the Scottish Secretary was impressed with the gravity of the situation. They clearly exaggerated the extent of the troubles, suggesting that thousands of munition workers were involved in the agitation and any evictions would almost certainly result in industrial action.[247] Yet there was little doubt that industrial support for the resistance was growing at the same period that shipbuilding and engineering workers were struggling against state repression. A powerful impetus to both forms of unrest was the determination of particular employers and landlords to force through changes against the advice of moderate officials and union leaders, even if industrial capitalists as a whole were uncertain of effective strategies. The unflinching initiative of one factor led to the prosecution of nine Partick rent strikers at the Small Debts Court on 12th October. Rosslyn Mitchell skilfully focussed on the case of Robert Duncan, a local munitions worker who would face impossible difficulties on eviction since he could neither take time off work nor secure a Clearance Certificate.[248] After the owner's counsel argued that such men were well able to pay the increases demanded, Mitchell retorted that these men were engaged in work of national importance and did not choose to work fourteen hours a day willingly. Even if they could afford the rent rises through long hours of overtime, they were reluctant to pay on a point of principle:[249]

They were not working for the proprietors of their houses. They were working for the purpose of turning out munitions.

Mitchell went on to indicate the serious consequences of attempted evictions of either munitions workers or the dependants of servicemen, offering a direct warning to visiting Cabinet ministers as well as Clydeside landlords. In the event the Sheriff decided to adjourn the cases involving six munitions workers, whilst granting ejectment warrants for three others — including one against Partick strike leader Andrew Hood.

On the 13th October the Govan Trades Council sent their telegram demanding the release of the shipwrights, and the next day it became widely known that Lloyd George intended to arrange for some form of official enquiry into rent levels. Despite the pleas of McKinnon Wood that landlords should 'stay their hand' until this investigation, Glasgow factors responded by an immediate notice of further rent rises. John Maclean's *Vanguard* was probably correct in claiming that the owners were trying to achieve a bargaining position with sizeable increases, in the hope that half the increase would be officially allowed later.[250] Disregarding the persistent calls of the tenants and Labour leaders that landlords should be regulated in the same way as workers, the propertied interests pressed ahead with their rises and justified every advance in the trade press.[251] It was against this background of renewed protests and the arrival of the Balfour-Macassey enquiry into Clyde munitions troubles (beginning its sittings on 15th October) that Glasgow Corporation again debated the problem of rent strikes.[252] There were reports that Lloyd George was considering resolving the deadlock by the provisions of the Munitions Act, and it was clear that his Ministry were desperately trying to head off the widespread unpopularity of the legislation by some conciliatory gesture.[253] In the City Chambers the councillors were sharply divided over the merits of the tenants' case, with a strong attack on 'certain agitators, some of whom were present in the Council' by a Conservative spokesman.[254] With noisy support from the Labour seats, John S. Taylor demanded an immediate enquiry by the Council into rent rises and pointed out that Lloyd George had only promised a 'fair rent court' (i.e. an enquiry), after the Govan tenants had threatened that if they were evicted then 'the men in the Fairfield Shipyard were to stop work'.[255] The Council refused to act until the Government initiative was known, and on 18th October McKinnon Wood announced the appointment of an official enquiry into alleged rent increases at munitions districts within Scotland.[256] It was to be headed by the eminent Scottish Advocate, Lord Hunter, who was decidedly sympathetic to houseowners suffering interest rate increases at the hands of bondholders and financial institutions.[257] He was joined by the Adam Smith professor of political economy at Glasgow University, Scott, who remained a committed disciple of the free market throughout a long career.[258]

This did nothing to deflect the steady advance of rent increases and legal contests during the last two weeks of October. The three warrants issued against three Partick rent strikers fell to be executed on Saturday 16th October,

Rent strikers at the Small Debts Court, 12th October 1915.

(Picture reproduced in *The Bulletin*, 13th October 1915.)

though one of the tenants (significantly a local policeman) left voluntarily. Andrew Hood had his wounded brother staying at his home when 2,000 people from Partick and Govan arrived to defend the two homes against the Sheriff's officers.[259] On the day, factors and officers failed to appear for it was widely recognised that the local workmen were available to offer 'strenuous opposition' against any attempted ejectment.[260] This tactical victory was offset by the reopening of the hearings against six munitions workers a few days later, when an unsympathetic Sheriff rejected Mitchell's plea that a relevant Committee of Enquiry was about to hear evidence, and the warrants were granted against these and a Parkhead man refusing rent payments.[261]

More importantly, the consequence of the wave of mid-October rent rises provoked by the rumours and reports of official intervention, raised the struggle to a new level as a wide variety of tenants found themselves the target of fresh increases. Local papers such as the *Govan Press* noted that munitions workers could probably afford the increases with little hardship, but in the same districts were families which had experienced a real decline in wages and income, for whom a 10% rise was a serious burden. Equally worrying was the prospect of further demands if tenants conceded extra rents now, and it was this general fear of housing monopoly that underlay the ferocity of the Autumn struggles.[262] The most vulnerable were the wives of men away on military service and despite assurances of the House Factors' Association that such groups would receive special consideration, Andrew Hood offered evidence of at least six cases where rent rises had been demanded of soldiers' wives or mothers.[263] Also under threat were the 8,000 old age pensioners living at Glasgow, Wheatley arguing in June 1915 that the 7,700 households recorded below the minimum-rates line could hardly afford the rent increases brought by War.[264] At the same time that moves were made to evict a munitions worker in South Govan on 20th October, Sheriff's officers attempted to enforce an eviction order against a pensioner of seventy at Partick.[265] According to Patrick Dollan, local shipyard workers arrived to protect the man against the authorities and threatened industrial action against evictions in the area.[266] A similar incident occurred near Govan Town Hall when a widow with a son in the local shipyards faced eviction by court order. Housewives from the Govan Women's Housing Association

"'The Battle of Partick.'" ::
Report from the Firing Line — "It's a' richt, Mrs M'Stinger, we've pit the Sheriff's Officer in the Washin' Hoose b'iler an' lichtit the fire." — Official.

Cartoon from *The Baillie*, October 1915.

were picketing the house when the officers appeared. The women immediately launched a vigorous barrage of peasemeal, flour and whiting against the invading force, with the result that one picket was arrested for assault. After negotiations with Mary Barbour and a consultation with the widow lying ill inside the house, the officers retreated from the scene of battle releasing their captive in the process.[267]

The character of the areas still involved in the strike was also significant, for though many immigrant workers in munitions production had been forced to take poor housing in the slum quarters of Anderston, Calton, Bridgeton and Mile-End, there had been virtually no increases in rent. Their fundamental problems remained those of bad accommodation unfit for human habitation, as Andrew McBride pointed out. The question of sizeable rent increases really arose 'in the better-class working localties' such as Govanhill where workers were compelled to break the law in resisting the factors.[268] In a survey conducted by Walker Smith of Glasgow rents, it was discovered that less than one quarter of housing had seen increases of more than 5% since the outbreak of War. Yet in the sample from central Govan, every house recorded rises in the range of 14%-23%, whilst the Fairfield district experienced increases of 12%-15% at the same time. It was evident that very high rents were being demanded in the districts surrounding the bustling shipbuilding and engineering works in the first year of War.[269] There were very large numbers of skilled 'munitions' workers in such areas, with David Wardley suggesting that most residents were employed by shipbuilding or the cooperative stores by 1915, though there were also many unskilled labourers who suffered from the general pattern of increases.[270] A similar situation existed in Partick, where Andrew Hood argued that any tenant not benefiting from increased wages at munitions work underwent real hardship as a result of the landlords' increases.[271]

Each of the main groups affected by rent rises felt a keen sense of injustice at the exactions, irrespective of particular ability to pay. Engineering and shipbuilding trades on munitions work, along with other occupations, objected to the advantage taken of their longer hours of work and higher income.[272] Employees such as the non-manual staff of foremen, draughtsmen and clerical workers had been subsisting on fixed salaries and without increases

GLASGOW LABOUR PARTY HOUSING COMMITTEE.

Great Protest DEMONSTRATION

AGAINST INCREASES OF RENTS

AND IN FAVOUR OF MUNICIPAL HOUSING

WILL BE HELD IN THE

CITY HALL,

On FRIDAY, 29th OCT , at 8 p.m.

Bailie JAMES STEWART in the Chair.

Doors open at 6-30 p.m. Organ Recital from 7 to 8 p.m.

WOMEN OF GLASGOW !

After two years' persistent work by our Housing Committee, the Women of Glasgow have at length realised that the Houseowners have the power to increase the Rents to a figure almost impossible for women to pay, and that the Law, which the people imagined was made by themselves, and for themselves, **does not protect their homes.**

Under these circumstances, our women, who have sacrificed so much to defend the country, have banded themselves together to **protect their homes.**

What they demand is—

"That the Government make illegal all increases of Rent imposed since the war started; that the Town Council, in view of the scarcity of Housing, proceed to erect Houses at the very earliest date, using the Tramway Surplus (Interest Free) for this purpose."

Gathering of the Clans!

RALLYING MEETING

Will be held on **WEDNESDAY, 27th OCTOBER, at 8 p.m.**

At **Corner of POLMADIE RD. and RUTHERGLEN RD.**

Addresses will be delivered and arrangements made for this district to reach

THE GREAT CITY HALL MEETING.

Bring the Factors' Missives! They will be solemnly burned at this Meeting.

Remember, you cannot be ejected on the 28th, when your tenancy expires. Therefore the party who takes your House must store their furniture in the street for 8 days until decree has been secured against you.

"Not Removing" Notices, 1d. each. Sold at Meeting.

Contemporary pamphlet.

Photograph reproduced in *The*

Bulletin. Friday, 8th October 1915.

commensurate to the extra effort required of them in Wartime. Groups in other industries not reaping the fruits of Government contracts and munitions work, including the host of professional or self-employed men and the shop-keeping groups, often faced serious difficulties as a result of the War and (like Andrew Hood) refused to pay extra rent on principle. Finally, dependants of active servicemen and the aged had frequently seen a fall in their standard of living as a result of rising prices and rents. The fixed incomes little above poverty level hardly permitted increased outlay on rent, many of these families actually falling into arrears with the factor by 1915.

The less powerful working class and professional recipients of rent increases and removal notices escaped the attention of press and Government, but the unmistake-able unrest amongst the shipyard and engine shop employees could not be ignored. It was in the first weeks of October that *The Times* began to carry reports of the Glasgow strikes, identifying the strategic districts of Partick and Springburn as centres of agitation.[273] Shortly after the prosecution of the rebellious shipwrights at Fairfields, the Govan branch of their Society sent a memorandum of protest to the Scottish Office, objecting to the 'abnormal increase in rents' imposed on Govan tenants and requesting the creation of Fair Rent Courts to arbitrate over local rent levels.[274] The question of rent increases came up at the Balfour-Macassey enquiry sitting during the week from 15th October, though the examination of Clyde unrest terminated without resolving the shipwrights' dispute, which boiled over once again on 23rd-27th October before Lloyd George could defuse the crisis.[275] On the 26th October, a shop steward from the strife-torn Weir plant at Cathcart was prosecuted before a Munitions Tribunal for allegedly assaulting another worker, attended by 300 workmates who carried him off on the dismissal of the case.[276]

This growing support in industry was strengthened by the increasing number of districts involved in the rents campaign during the latter weeks of October. Following the successful grant of eviction warrants at the trial of the six Partick munitions workers, landlords engaged in another wave of rent rises around the city. The neighbouring district of Whiteinch rallied to the rent strike, whilst Cathcart and Kinning Park set up tenants' strike committees by the end of the month.[277] Shettleston again achieved notoriety as a centre of resistance under the leadership of a local tenant and sustained by the speeches of Stewart, Kerr and Wheatley.[278] In each case trades unions and trades councils offered practical and fraternal support to the rent strikers, with Glasgow Trades Council receiving the Cathcart Tenants' Committee and upon the insistence of activists such as Shinwell and Laidlaw the Trades delegates resolved that no trade unionist should 'take a house from which a Tenant has been evicted'.[280] Outstanding in the organisation of the Cambuslang strike was Owen Coyle of the Iron and Steel union, who invited Trades Councillors as well as Labour Party leaders to encourage the initiatives of the tenant committees.[281] Yet the immediate direction of local campaigns and the initial impetus for organisation seems to have remained with tenant leaders involved in the neighbourhood. Mrs Nixon and the Glasgow Women's Housing Association were certainly evident in the mobilisation of Maryhill tenants, but the decision to resist began with the residents.[282] When addressing the tenants' association under O'Donnel, one speaker from the Trades Council and the Labour Party emphasised that:[283]

... this agitation was not instituted by the Labour Party, who never interfered unless there was a direct appeal from the tenants themselves ... they had no less than 35 appeals from tenants in Maryhill.

The bitterness provoked by the sweeping rent increases of mid-October, also hardened opinion against the landlords and made compromise solutions much more difficult. Previous demands for official enquiries and fair rents courts had now given way to an insistence on the prohibition of all Wartime rent rises, and the threat of further direct action against the unacceptable proposals of any such enquiry. Owen Coyle told the Cambuslang strikers that they were not waiting upon the result of any Commission of Enquiry, whilst Mrs Ferguson told the Partick activists that their position was so strong that they would be:[284]

able to refuse to accept the decision of the Commissioners appointed to conduct the Government inquiry, if they considered the terms harsh.

No doubt the conduct of the Commission to enquire into industrial unrest, which had departed on 21st October without the release of imprisoned shipwrights, had eroded popular faith in the efficacy of such government appointees.

It was against this background of continuing industrial conflict and widespread distrust of state departments, that the Hunter-Scott enquiry opened at Glasgow on 26th October. In view of the growing urgency of the rents problem throughout Scotland, the chairmen took evidence from the landlords, strike leaders and officials for only three days before leaving for Dundee and Aberdeen on the 30th October. The Committee found that there was little evidence of widespread and substantial increases since the outbreak of War to match the image of 'profit huns' painted on socialist platforms, but about the depth of tenant resistance there could be no doubt. Owners and factors adopted a fairly defensive stance in their contributions, emphasising the burdens of interest rates and repairs during this period of general shortages in capital, labour and materials. The landlord press continued to inveigh against the actions of an 'irresponsible clique which has, for purposes of reprehensible progaganda, formed a no-rent strike and encouraged revolt', but even here there were fewer spokesmen willing to argue that the state could not interfere with the laws of market demand.[285] On their side, the tenant and Labour leaders emphasised the general crisis of housing provision under private enterprise, as well as the specific threat which landlord opportunism posed to efficient munitions production. Thus Andrew Hood told the Committee that the families able to shoulder the increased rents were precisely the munitions workers who objected to the advantage taken of their high earnings.[286] Hence the local press agreed that most tenants even in Partick were not enjoying the extraordinary wages paid to shipyard workers, despite the difficulties faced through Wartime increases.[287] It was on a wider question of legitimate increases to offset increased costs that Lord Hunter attempted to draw Andrew McBride, suggesting that a fair and reasonable appraisal must allow owners a basic return on investment. McBride replied in terms that outlined the practical policies of the Labour Party Housing Committee, whilst rejecting the assumption that allowances should be made for the immediate difficulties imposed by market capitalism on houseowners:[288]

We argue that rents are too high. It does not matter what causes bring about high rents; we say that they can be

changed, so that . . . if the system cannot be worked by private enterprise, then they must go by the board and bring houses within reach of the working class.

The eminent legal writer and the professor of classical economics must have found such expressions disturbing, even if they were impressed by the sheer scale of the opposition to private landlords in Autumn 1915.

This range of resistance and organisation clearly could not be explained by reference to the rent rises — or even fears of future exactions — alone, and as the enquiry progressed it became clear that the rents campaign had harnessed a diversity of grievances and protests. Working class housewives and lower-middle class groups on fixed salaries found that they were suffering increases in basic foodstuffs, as well as in rents and taxes, during the first year of War. Andrew Hood commented in his evidence that sudden rent rises was not the major problem, but that with 'the pressure being brought to bear . . . on us in other directions, we feel the gradual increase in rent now all the more keenly'.[289] The high price of food and other necessaries remained probably the most important factor in working class unrest during the War, but the scope for attacks or boycotts on individual shopkeepers (themselves possibly suffering from rent increases) was decidedly limited. When questioned as to the strength of feeling on the rents question, Andrew Hood made this quite clear in arguing that:[290]

We hold that we cannot deal with the grocer and the baker as we are in a position to deal with the factor. My position is this, that if we could get at the root of the evil, so far as food is concerned . . . we would strike as well against the one as the other.

The general feeling that any increases in such essential items at a time of emergency was unjustified and unpatriotic, also involved an important moral imperative which developed into a sustained attack on 'profiteering' during the War years. It was this sense of outrage and indignation at the eviction of soldiers' dependants and munitions workers engaged in the War effort, that was articulated in the banners carried by rent strikers to the court hearings at Glasgow and elsewhere. Many strike spokesmen were the self-employed men of talent attracted to the I.L.P. and other parties, who were able to afford the advances demanded at Partick or Govan but who saw their resistance as 'largely a fight on principle'.[291] In response to this persistent and popular denunciation of landlords as unscrupulous and unpatriotic profiteers, Glasgow owners conceded the claim that no dependant of servicemen should be evicted for refusing rent. But such attempts at magnanimity came too late to reverse the distinct shift in public sympathy against the property owners, as reflected in both local and national press reports.[292]

By the time Hunter and Scott left for Dundee at the end of October, the rent strikers had gained a powerful position in Glasgow. In the words of one *Forward* article, they had achieved three objectives: compelling house factors to give a public guarantee that the rents of dependants would not be raised, forcing the Government to investigate and report on the rent problem, and preventing the ejectment warrants against strikers being enforced. The Labour weekly added, that the 'fourth point still to be won is the establishment of pre-War rents', which had replaced the long-standing demand for fair rents tribunals as the primary objective of the tenants' campaign.[293] The events of the following three weeks translated this demand into Government policy, as ministers were confronted with fresh signs of industrial disruption and tenant mobilisation.

On the departure of the rents committee chairmen, there were reports of continuing rent strikes in areas as distinct as Anderston, central Govan, Govanhill and Polmadie, coordinated again by Labour organisations and tenant committees.[294] There was greater calm on the industrial front as Bridges was acquitted and the shipwrights released from gaol, so that the Balfour-Macassey enquiry resumed its sitting in a reasonably tranquil situation on 4th November.[295] At the same time, however, supporters were building closer links between the areas of struggle at Glasgow and beyond Clydeside. In early November the local War Emergency Committee requested the support of Glasgow Trades Council in organising a protest against the action of landlords in raising rents, though the delegates side-stepped the issue by passing the matter over to Andrew McBride and the Labour Party.[296] About the same time, Ben Shaw of the Glasgow Party was writing to Middleton at the War Emergency Workers' National Committee, explaining the advance of tenant demands beyond the Party's call for Fair Rent Courts and the 'most emphatic and unanimous pronouncement' instead for pre-War rents.[297] Though the

National Committee included such luminaries as Mary Macarthur, Margaret Bondfield, Susan Lawrence and Robert Smillie, it was generally in the rear of the rents movement (as contrasted with their promotion of the food question), only gradually becoming aware of widespread dissatisfaction over the subject in the Autumn crisis.[298] The more dramatic proposal of John Maclean that the Trades Council should organise a 'general strike' at Glasgow to oppose the landlords and achieve rent restriction, was shelved without debate by the delegates at this point.[299]

Despite this setback, Maclean and his B.S.P. comrades channelled their energies into factory and shipyard gate meetings in support of the rent strikes, attracting attention for their anti-War views at the same time in these dinner-hour gatherings.[300] The I.L.P.ers like Hopkins continued their fight for workplace reinforcements as well, and during the second week of November *Forward* was able to report that 'emergency Committees' in the various shipyards and workshops had been established around Partick, in support of the rent strike, noting that:[301]

Dinner-hour meetings have been held during the week, and the munitions men have promised financial and other support. The Trade Union branches ought to interest themselves in this question.

It is significant that the shipyards were building emergency committees in support of campaigns such as rent strikes at the same time that Kirkwood and other engineering stewards were developing the Clyde Trades Vigilance Committee (later the Clyde Workers' Committee). Industrial employers frequently encouraged the creation of 'war relief funds' in their works, which drew collections from the workmen and distributed rent subsidies to the dependants of servicemen under the direction of employees themselves, though they usually avoided becoming more directly involved in the housing and rents controversies.[302]

Under mounting pressure from tenants and public criticism, as well as the reports of parallel rent strikes throughout the United Kingdom by November, Glasgow's landlords made a last desperate effort to secure increases and reassert their authority. One large Partick factor, Daniel Nicholson, applied for warrants of eviction against eighteen tenants after they refused a 2s. per month (upon a rental of almost £2 a month or 10s. per week) increase in rent. Many of the householders were shipyard workers at Beardmore's Dalmuir yard, unable to secure accommodation nearer their place of work. Since the factor advised prosecution in the Small Debts Court at Glasgow, it was possible to order a deduction of the amounts owed from the wages of the employees at their work, provided the Sheriff was prepared to direct the repayment of increases as a debt.[303] After the defendants received their summons to court for the 17th November, a large demonstration was organised by the Glasgow Women's Housing Association on the 13th. As contingents of women, men and children poured in from Partick, Whiteinch and Scotstoun, a platform was established at Thornwood Hill overlooking the Clyde shipyards. The crowd listend to Councillor Izett and Ben Smith as well as Mrs Ferguson of the G.W.H.A., but it was Helen Crawfurd who dominated the meeting with her powerful rhetoric — telling the assembled supporters that:[304]

this fight was essentially a woman's fight. All who were taking part in the demonstration were showing their solidarity. They were asking not for money, not for charity; they were asking for justice. . . . She respected all laws that were just and fair, but she did not ask them to respect the law which allowed increases in rents to be enforced at the present juncture.

Arrangements were made to ensure that a large contingent should accompany the Partick strikers to court four days later, turning the stuffy courtroom into a celebration of working class values and protests.

News reached London of this impending legal battle, and on the day before the case was due to be heard the factor's solicitor received a letter from Lloyd George himself, requesting that he either drop the prosecution or postpone the proceedings 'with a view to allowing the legislation that was promised to come into force'.[305] This was sufficient to persuade the petitioners, though the Tenants' Defence Committee led by James Reid of the Dalmuir yard, seized the initiative and insisted that the cases should be heard as scheduled or dropped altogether.[306] This the factor would not do and the trial went ahead as planned, with thousands of women, workers and children streaming into George Square to surround the court entrance. At least five major shipyards and one armaments works struck work in support of the defendants, though a number of other plants — including key engineering works around Clydeside — sent deputations to express solidarity with the rent strike.[307] From makeshift platforms on the back of trailers or converted from wooden doors, speakers such as Mary Barbour, Andrew McBride, Jimmy MacDougall and John Maclean addressed the crowds surging around the City Chambers.[308] Inside the crowded courtroom there was considerable delay as the case scheduled for 10.00 a.m. had still not been heard at noon, whereupon Councillor Izett came forward to protest 'in the name of the people' at the lethargy of Sheriff Lee. This brought an irate, if not unsympathetic, sheriff from his chambers with the threat to clear the court if order was not maintained. Before the case was heard, however, representatives of the various workers' contingents appealed for a private audience with Sheriff Lee, which he granted in view of the extraordinary circumstances of the case and the direct threat to the Government's War effort. One spokesman from the Beardmore yard at Dalmuir claimed that its 8,000 workers were on the point of striking in support of the rent strikers, but decided to send a deputation instead. He suggested that the factors should be 'charged under the Defence of the Realm Act', and his arguments were reinforced by a speaker from 'one of the principal Engine Shops on the Clyde' who warned that the men 'were red hot, and the only way to avoid trouble was to have the cases dropped'. Another spokesman from the stronghold of the rent strikes at Govan assured Lee that he was dealing with a sustained struggle rather than a spasmodic movement.[4Å0] The beleaguered judge pleaded for moderation, insisting that it was not his decision that would weigh with the Government but the 'horrible thought of industrial strife bringing untold misery into our midst'.[310] Having failed to convince the deputations of the wisdom of continuing the cases pending the Cabinet's decision on legislation, the Sheriff returned to the packed courtroom.

In the tense excitement of the chamber, Reid agreed that his own defence was to be the 'test case' for the fifteen warrants affecting munitions workers but flatly refused to consider an adjournment. Well aware of the pressure which such workers could place on the Minister of Munitions, Reid skilfully argued that the fifteen men:[311]

did not wish to stay off work to come there and discuss the

question of rent. They had a bigger battle to fight in the workshops and they wanted to fight loyally there.

After the Tenants' Defence Committee were consulted, they again decided that there must be an immediate decision on their cases.[312] The Sheriff then turned to the prosecuting solicitor and after some hesitation, the cases were finally dropped. The owners and factors had lost in their last bid to assert legal supremacy over the rent strikers. After praising the benevolence of the owners and requesting safe conduct for the prosecution through the thousands of demonstrators, the Sheriff closed the case to the sound of prolonged cheering from the gallery.[313] Outside, the news was received with excited jubilation and from one of the platforms John Maclean proposed a public motion that, 'this meeting of Clyde munition workers requests the Government to definitely state . . . that it forbids any increase of rent during the period of the war'. It was carried by acclamation and the crowds wound their way back through Glasgow to Partick, Govan and even distant Dalmuir, convinced of success.[314]

The victory in the courts on 17th November did not mark the end of the rents campaign, still less the conclusion of working class struggle on the housing and prices issues. The reports carried of the great demonstration in papers such as *The Manchester Guardian,* did make a deep impression on London politicians, however, as did the reports of 20,000 tenants on rent strike in the Glasgow area by November 1915. Within two days of the court case, Labour M.P.s such as Will Thorne, W. C. Anderson and George Barnes were insisting that McKinnon Wood and his Cabinet colleagues take up the question as a matter of urgency.[135] Anderson had been elected to the Attercliffe division of Sheffield after the outbreak of War, standing as a moderate opponent of the War and in close touch with working class issues through his membership of Glasgow I.L.P. and his marriage to Mary Macarthur.[316] Particularly strong on the food question and other problems discussed in the War Emergency Workers' National Committee, Anderson contributed regular reports on Birmingham and other rent strikes, writing in *Forward* of the November 1915 events, that:[317]

The Glasgow tenants have learned one quite sound lesson.

They have discovered, thanks mainly to the teachings of the Labour men in Glasgow, that Governments help those who help themselves. Accept injustice meekly, and nothing will be done; resist it strongly and everything else will be added unto you.

The clear evidence of rents unrest throughout industrial Britain in the Autumn of 1915, finally convinced a reluctant Government that it could not dismiss the strike campaign as a phenomenon peculiar to Glasgow or that its threat to munitions production was limited to the Clydeside region.[318] There were serious rent troubles within Scotland at Aberdeen and Dundee, even though they had not witnessed munitions immigration on anything like a comparable scale to Clydeside.[319] Here also there were important links between the local Labour organisations and Trades Councils and the growing support enjoyed by the rent strikers.[320] There were significant rent protests recorded at Birmingham, Birkenhead, London, Belfast and Northampton during October and November of 1915, widely reported in the Labour and bourgeois newspapers.[321] One Belfast campaign had been abandoned after a compromise in October, whilst the Birmingham strike was declared a success on the same day that the Glasgow munitions workers appeared in court.[322] As *Forward* told its readers, the rent issue was 'now a national question and must be settled nationally', though its particular forms and objectives differed between distinct localities.[323]

Among the more prominent contributors to the rents struggles were the London districts such as Woolwich, Edmonton, Tooting, and Poplar. The Woolwich context paralleled that of Clydebank or Govan in many respects, having a tradition of independent labour politics dating back to 1903 and even 1898.[324] Government munitions works and torpedo production at the Arsenal gave the borough a vital strategic significance as well as a strong contingent of skilled workers who developed their own cooperative and building societies autonomous from bourgeois control.[325] As at Glasgow and Govan, the Labour Representation Association formed in 1903 mobilised around the ward committees under the leadership of William Barefoot and C. H. Grinling.[326] There also flourished a strong current of labour and socialist journalism, as the *Woolwich Pioneer* grew out of the earlier *Labour Notes* and *Journals* under the influence of Barefoot and his 'Freelance' contributions to the weekly paper.[327] Such publications enjoyed the support of skilled manual workers as well as unskilled labour, clerical employees, professional and supervisory grades, and others.[328] Woolwich was therefore one of the few areas, along with Glasgow and Merthyr, able to sustain a Labour weekly to complement the appeal of the national *Labour Leader.*[329]

Woolwich resembled munitions areas of Clydeside also, in the evidence it offered of growing industrial discontent during 1914-15 — including that among the supervisory employees responsible for discipline in the key workshops.[330] Rents protests were also reported as early as December 1914, encouraged by the *Pioneer* and its slogan of 'War on War Rents and the Rapacity of Rack Renters'. Memories of housing shortages and rent rises during the hectic production of the Boer War, spurred many tenants into direct resistance and a flurry of complaints via the Labour Party and its newspaper to the National Emergency Committee.[331] In April 1915 there was a fresh upsurge of resistance as rent increases were demanded from local landlords, with a number of tenants contacting Barefoot about a possible Tenants' Defence League and which he then promoted in the *Pioneer* columns.[332] This prompted a committed response from Ada Jennings at Plumstead, whose letter to 'Freelance' betrays a strong political awareness of capitalist exploitation. Her correspondence documented individual cases of hardship in the area, including the eviction of some Arsenal policemen and one man on active service in the Army. Mrs Jennings pointed out the bitter irony of munitions workers having to spend their scarce leisure hours in house-hunting, and offered to form a tenants' association, adding that:[333]

I have given addresses in different parts of the district for some time past on the housing question and should like to see a crusade got up against the modern landlord and his unscrupulous ways . . . but only united effort will tell.

The local Trades Council and Labour organisations again moved in to support the protean Defence League in June 1915, advising local tenants to refuse rent increases and wait upon landlord or state initiatives.[334] Addison and his advisers at the Ministry of Munitions acted quickly to establish the Well Hall Estate at Woolwich, housing hundreds of essential munitions workers and relieving some of the pres-

The Town Council Scandal

OPEN LETTER

To the Citizens of Glasgow

Fellow Citizens,

Mr. Brown of the "Herald League" paid Mr. Freer £1 deposit for the City Hall for a **DEMONSTRATION AGAINST CONSCRIPTION on Monday, November 29.** The contract was closed in writing. Bills and posters were printed and issued, then, to the surprise of the responsible Committee, Mr. Freer returned the money and stated that the engagement was cancelled.

The Labour Party in the Town Council raised the matter so vigorously that Councillor George Kerr was suspended. All honour to him!

The Council is responsible if the hall is not open on Monday for the Demonstration.

In view of the turn of events the Free Speech Defence Committee now takes full responsibility for the conduct of affairs.

The Demonstration will go on in the City Hall on Monday first, November 29, at 7.45 p.m.

Doors must be open at 7 p.m.

Speakers—GEORGE LANSBURY, SYLVIA PANKHURST, JAMES MAXTON, M.A., etc.

Chairman—JOHN MACLEAN.

Admission Free. **Reserved Seats, 6d.**

Whether you favour the purpose of the meeting or not, come and show your determination not to allow the Council to introduce "Prussian" methods.

FREE SPEECH DEFENCE COMMITTEE.

N.B.—Arrangements have been made that the Speakers will appear and speak on SUNDAY FIRST at the Meetings in the Pavilion, the Metropole and the Panoptican to prepare for Monday's event.

Pamphlet reflecting in its speakers the interconnectedness of Rent and War issues.

Glasgow Labour Party Housing Committee.

GOVAN DISTRICT.

Great Public

PROCESSION

AND

DEMONSTRATION

Of Rent Strikers, Trade Unionists, and Sympathisers,

ON

Saturday first, 27th November.

Procession

Will be fotmed at Lorne Square at 2-30, and will proceed through the principal Streets, to Maxwell Park, So. Govan, where a Monstre Demonstration will be held.

RESOLUTION to be moved and supported by Prominent Speakers:—

"That we, the Tenants in the Govan District of Glasgow demand that the Government shall establish PRE-WAR RENTS and force the Housefactors to return to Tenants all increases paid since the War started."

Men and Women of Govan,—Take your place in the procession and thus register your demand.

Pamphlet for meeting referred to opposite.

sure on available dwellings. Influenced by earlier ventures in company housing as well as contemporary ideologies of 'garden city planning', Well Hall suburb appears as a timely exercise in state housing intervention which contributed to Government strategies on accommodating labour.[335]

Impressive though such commitments were, they were necessarily limited in their scale and scope at a period when regions such as Clydeside faced a fundamental crisis in housing supply. Thus when George Barnes and Will Thorne (the latter Member of the Labour seat of West Ham), confronted the Government on the rents question in mid-October, they were assured by Addison that the state was committed to the provision of 45,000 additional dwellings to which Thorne could reply:[336]

That's far ahead. If it was a question of these men stopping away from work you would quickly deal with them.

It was this awareness of Government acting only under considerable pressure that convinced the Glasgow strikers of the need to maintain the initiative after the court case of 17th November. Tenants at areas such as Govan entered a period of almost constant mobilisation and demonstration, with a large procession from South Govan to the burgh Town Hall under George Galloway and the L.R.C. to urge the Labour Party (in Parliament and without), to ensure that the promised legislation should include a clause establishing pre-War rents.[337] George Barnes and W. C. Anderson had forced an assurance from the Government front bench on 18th November of the intention to legislate quickly and all efforts were now turned to guarantee a favourable Act.[338] On 27th November the Govan section of Labour's Housing Committee organised another large procession to Maxwell Park, where they demanded the restoration of pre-War rents and the return of all rent increases levied by factors since the outbreak of the War.[339] At such gatherings popular campaigners of the rent strikes that had begun months previously, such as Mary Barbour and councillors Denny, Dollan, Sharp and Wardley, insisted on the need for better housing as well as reasonable rents and encouraged the activists to remain in the organisations until these were secured.[340]

On 25th November, President of the Local Government Board and Tory squire Walter Long introduced a Bill into the Commons to restrict rents and mortgage interest on working class housing in munitions districts. Long frankly admitted that the legislation had been introduced because of a very deep feeling of bitterness and resentment against landlords, which 'is a danger to society and ought to be removed'.[341] The majority of speakers agreed with the minister, though a handful of Members (including the M.P. for the City of London) attacked the Bill as an unprincipled surrender to outside pressure — to which Long made an angry reply.[342] He was supported by Liberals such as Mackinder, who argued that the demand for, and regulation of, labour under exceptional conditions necessitated a similar restriction of housing and other market commodities in the interest of the state as a whole.[343] Even Tudor Walter, representing the owners and bondholders as the backbone of private housing and defending their position against the claims of financial and other capitalists at a time of rising interest rates, welcomed the measure.[344] The larger landed interests who were directly involved in the profits accruing from working class housing at many cities, had earlier realised the dangers of social upheaval and made a direct appeal for moderation in the increase of rent.[345] With thousands of small owners pressing for a relaxation of interest charges and industrial employers concerned at continuing unrest, the balance of support had shifted in favour of reform by this point.

The propertied interests and bourgeois politicians had also learned enough from the bitter industrial conflicts and rent strikes of 1915 to avoid some of the obvious pitfalls in the framing of the legislation. In the course of the rents resistance the demand for pre-War rents superseded the calls for 'fair rents tribunals' and for an immediate investigation into increases. Working class experience of tribunals under the Defence of Realm Act and Munitions legislation served to undermine the previous popularity of legal contests against the landlords. Pre-War struggles against evictions had offered a training ground for socialist advocates such as Rossyln Mitchell, whilst the creation of a Fair Rent Court in Ireland had permitted a sustained attack on the unscrupulous practices of British and native landlords.[346] Thus the principle of fair rents tribunals still carried a particular resonance in the tenant movement, which was quickly taken up by the Liberal Mackinder in his attack upon those using the rents campaign to 'advocate the housing of people on a totally different footing'. Referring to the suggestion that a fair rent court should be established to arbitrate over future rent levels, this shrewd parliamentarian observed that:[347]

Every resort to a Court . . . gives an opportunity for dispute and gives an opportunity to these propagandists — hold what opinions we like in times of peace, we want to silence them in times of war — to maintain irritation.

Here lay the significance of the debate surrounding the precise conditions under which the new legislation was to be administered, given the scope for continuing controversy in key industrial districts. Questions were raised as to the annual rental of the houses to be covered under the Bill, with George Barnes suggesting that almost 90% of Glasgow housing (198,400 of 222,000) would be covered by the proposed £21 per annum rental.[348] Eventually this was raised so that every tenant paying £30 or less in rent had his outlay restricted for at least six months beyond the end of the War, which protected the host of professional, shopkeeping and independent groups who also suffered from rent interest increases at this time.[349] There were also difficulties in the delineation of 'munitions districts' and industrial centres, so that the proposal to limit the operation of the Act to cities over 100,000 people gave way (again under pressure) to a rent restriction covering the whole country.

It was in the search for a balance between interest and expediency that most politicians and opinion-makers united in the weeks of Parliamentary debate. Thus one *Times* leader agreed that the measure was justified only by the exigencies of War, though acknowledging the moral force of a campaign which had attracted numerous clergymen to its ranks and which rallied its supporters on the principles of justice and patriotism. Leaving the situation in the hands of people well able to offer passive resistance had the merits of a 'laissez faire' neutrality from government, but also endangered the war effort by its development into active hostility against landlords.[350] Yet even the most eloquent speech or editorial could not disguise the violation of fundamental bourgeois principles by a measure which was 'illogical and unsound on grounds of political economy'.[351] It was this aspect which was taken up by George Barnes in his sardonic congratulation of Long on the introduction of the Bill, emphasising that:[352]

It is a matter for congratulation that the House has, almost with one accord, agreed to the demise of political economy.

Political economy or unlimited competition has had a fairly long and, I think, dishonourable life. It has enabled dealers in monopoly values to enrich themselves at the expense of the community.

However much Long might deny that his Bill was a concession to any class in the community or to the fear of social upheaval, the reluctance and delay of Government action had deprived it of real moral authority even amongst its supporters.[353] At the beginning of December the Bill received a second reading before being rushed through the Commons less than ten days before Christmas.

After the considerable concessions were made on the second reading of the Bill, tenant leaders at Glasgow agreed to accept the legislation and the famous rent strike notices began to disappear from the windows of working class tenements.[354] Although the Government had accepted that there should be no victimisation of rent strikers and that only the nonpayment of customary rents or serious misconduct should be grounds for eviction, the question remained of liablity for increases levied since the outbreak of War.[355] Some rent strike leaders urged the continuation of resistance to secure the repayment of rent increases already collected, though their support was obviously limited to the few districts where high rents had been successfully implemented over the previous year.[356] The importance of the rents victory should not obscure the real limitations of the Autumn legislation. There was to be no return of increases collected since the beginning of War, nor any system of rent courts to ascertain a fair rent in existing housing. The legal powers of the owners and factors on evictions remained untouched, and ejectments for nonpayment of earlier rents and misconduct continued in Scotland on a massive scale for the remainder of the War.[357] Even more important, there was no legal obligation on the Government to deal with the underlying housing crisis which had precipitated the rents controversy and the Royal Commission on Housing in Scotland remained in abeyance until the following year. Only the continuing severity of depression in the housebuilding industry, coupled with the resurgence of industrial and social protest around the housing question, compelled the state to undertake housing on a significant scale in 1919-21. Though there developed a serious challenge to the political and moral authority of a militarised state, there was no sustained attack by the rent strikers, on either the Munitions legilsation or the property and authority relations which underpinned its control, after November 1915.

CHAPTER TEN

Clydeside labour: implications of the rents struggle

The greatest strength of the rents campaign at Clydeside and elsewhere, was its success in encompassing a wide range of grievances and organisations under the banner of fair rents. Yet the movement against the landlords was itself only part of a much wider struggle for the provision and administration of basic services required by working class families. Just as pre-War and Wartime industrial conflicts touched upon the underlying issue of workplace control, so the tenants' demands related to a broader class contest over the character and control of social amenities at the point of consumption. The local committees of the War Emergency Workers' National Committee were particularly important in this respect, demanding a basic £1 per week allowance for widows and war dependants and including women as well as local labour bodies in its own membership.[358] After the struggle between the T.U.C. and National Committee over the composition of these local agencies, the T.U.C. was able to secure the promotion of Labour councillors rather than directly-elected activists or trade unionists in the selection.[359] Even so, the local committees remained significant forums for discussion of amenities as well as the administration of relief, especially where they built up strong links with the district Trades Councils.[360] They were at least able to ensure that the worst features of discrimination and stigma attached to the post-Victorian social services were minimised in administration. Hardship caused by rent arrears and increases during 1914-15 helps to explain the prominence of the National Committee in the public debate at London from October 1915 onwards.[361] At the same period, industrial workers were careful to keep the control of their workplace 'war relief funds' from the hands of astute or well-meaning employers, paying rent relief in areas like South Govan with little assistance from shipyard or engineering managements.[362]

An even more explicit example of the struggles taking place over social provisions came with the disciplining of

John Maclean for his activities in the Govan School Board. On the day following the trial of the Partick rent strikers at the Small Debts Court, Harry Hopkins appeared before the Board to complain of a disciplinary enquiry into the work of Maclean in helping to organise Govan's teaching staff. Despite the heroic efforts of Hopkins and others of the local Trades Council, the Board succeeded in suspending and eventually dismissing Maclean from his post as teacher.[363] But by that time he had already committed his whole life to Marxist education and agitation amongst Clyde shop stewards and working people, including the relentless peace campaign which ultimately brought his trial and imprisonment later in the War.[364]

Maclean and the B.S.P. *Vanguard* had been critical of the reluctance of the trade unions and even C.W.C. to become directly identified with the rent demands and what Maclean described as 'the first step towards the Political Strike' against the Government.[365] Similar divisions became all too apparent in December 1915 and early 1916, as the C.W.C. sought to devise a coherent munitions dilution programme whilst trade union officials struggled to negotiate a general agreement with the Government.[366] The rent strikes had exposed the divisions and antagonisms within the ranks of different propertied groups, as well as a lingering suspicion between industrial employers and the Munitions Ministry. The events of Winter 1915-16, however, provided the basis upon which a new accommodation between capital and the state (in alliance with sections of Labour and trade union leadership) could be cemented. Under pressure to devise a practicable dilution policy, the C.W.C. refused to adopt either an industry-wide programme of industrial unionism and workplace accountability or to oppose the War in terms demanded by Maclean and the B.S.P. Relations continued tense between stewards and officials in the unions, as the latter largely accepted Government assurances on payments and substitution. The engineering and shipbuilding tradesmen were themselves uncertain and divided over the implications of dilution, particularly when individual shop agreements were open for negotiation. After their futile and humiliating visit to Clydeside at Christmas 1915, therefore, Lloyd George and the dilution officials determined upon a decisive course of action.

The main obstacle facing the Dilution Commissioners now charged with the rapid implementation of workplace reorgansiation, was to gain the confidence and full support of industrialists undecided about any policy short of outright repression and conscription of union activists. Having persuaded Kirkwood and the Parkhead stewards to devise plant arrangements for dilution, the Commissioners were still unable to convince many industrialists of the urgency of the task. The most difficult to convince were the shipbuilders who had stood at the centre of many of the worst industrial and social conflicts of 1915, and whose complex work processes were not conducive to the radical simplification of tasks achieved in shell production or basic lathe work. Yet the state officials were equally determined that output should be rapidly increased in both sectors, with Lynden, Macassey (joint chairman of the Commission on Industrial Unrest) telling the Clyde Shipbuilders before the Parkhead crisis burst upon the scene, that:[367]

. . . the provisions of the Munitions Act would be fully enforced. All customs — demarcation or trade traditions — opposed to the introduction of unskilled and female labour . . . would be abrogated . . . nothing would be left undone to increase production.

The Commissioners also had very full powers under the Defence of the Realm Act regulations.

Once the Scheme was in operation there would be no turning back. The full weight of the Munitions Act would be enforced in case of opposition. It was imperative however . . . that the Commissioners should have the full and loyal support of the Employers in order to command success.

Two days later the quarrel between Kirkwood and the Beardmore management deteriorated into a full-scale stoppage over the operation of the Parkhead dilution agreement, and the Government were called upon to honour their earlier promises of full support. The subsequent deportation of some C.W.C. leaders and crushing of the resistance to engineering dilution was not unpredictable given the ruthless commitment of the state to its industrial strategy. Lacking a broad base of support and easily identified as militant activists, the C.W.C. could not hope to challenge the Munitions Ministry in the way that the rent strikers or even Fairfield shipwrights had done.

Thus the impetus created by the rents struggle, or the

convergence of issues around the question, did not ensure the success of subsequent workplace campaigns. Yet the experience of the tenant strikes did have an important legacy in terms of working class attitudes and labour organisations. On the industrial front, the various 'vigilance committees' and supportive deputations which were developed during the Summer and Autumn of 1915 clearly contributed to the evolution of local representation in the shipbuilding sector as well as engine shops. During the period of renewed crisis during early 1916, one member of the Boilermakers' Society told a gathering of Partick shipbuilding tradesman, that:[368]

Organisation was one of the strongest factors in life, and if they did not organise they would soon go to the wall. Let them take the rent strike as an example of how the women folks could organise. The men laughed the idea of a rent strike to scorn, but the women were determined and they won a glorious victory.

One of the most promising aspects of the resurrection of the Clyde Workers' Committee later in the War, was not just its greater support and popularity but the positive relations which were built up with the Glasgow Labour Party.[369] Rather than being imprisoned in the sectarian politics of the revolutionary parties, the Clyde Workers' Defence Committee went on to make important practical and theoretical contributions to the parallel debates on workshop democracy and the social programme of Reconstruction. Like George Barnes at an earlier period, Harry Hopkins was so successful in his campaigns inside the A.S.E. that he had become Glasgow District Secretary by the end of the War — in time to lead the famous 40 Hours Strike of 1919 for which he was subsequently disciplined and dismissed by his union.

Although there were 25,000 tenants reported to be on rent strike (including many who had not been issued with notices of increase) by November 1915, only a small minority continued as activists after the introduction of rent restrictions.[370] The passage of legislation made the revival of private enterprise and speculative building for sale to landlords even less likely, thereby contributing to an unavoidable housing shortage after the War.[371] This was the contradiction in which the Liberal politicians were caught during 1915: political expediency demanded immediate intervention and yet burdened the housebuilding industry with the certainty of low returns from working class accommodation. It also made the removal of restrictions a sensitive issue during the years when mass democracy and women's votes promised to change the character of parliamentary elections.[372] Labour Party spokesmen such as Andrew McBride, John Wheatley and Patrick Dollan realised the implications of the problems identified by the 1917 Report of the Royal Commission on Housing in Scotland, which correctly interpreted the housing question as one facing national governments rather than municipal authorities. The battles of 1915 had not resulted in any commitment to public housing beyond the munition workers' dwellings, and in extending his Labour Party Housing Committee from a Glasgow to a Scottish base, McBride hoped to rally widespread support for the Labour Programme. Like the moves towards greater workers' control in industry, these initiatives provoked internal divisions within the tenants' movement though one of the significant features of the post-War struggles was the participation of industrial workers in the campaign for better housing.[373]

Perhaps more important than the broad umbrella organisations promoted by the Labour Party, was the skeletal framework of local tenant groups and associations which survived the success of rent restriction. Bodies such as Mary Barbour's Govan Women's Housing Association retained their autonomy from the larger Glasgow and Scottish groups, as the did the array of tenant agencies which had flourished in the local areas. It was their presence which gave enquiries such as the (second) Hunter Committee of 1919, pause for thought when considering the case for the removal of rent restrictions after the War.[374] The pressures which the whole housing movement placed on government necessitated the introduction of Addison's legislation in 1919, providing central subsidies from the Exchequer for local authority building. Its objective contribution to the massive housing problems in Scotland was little more than marginal, since only 4,500 dwellings of the 57,000 needed had been completed by 1921.[375] Only the rise of a Labour Government and a fresh basis for subsidies under John Wheatley as Minister of Health, guaranteed a sustained housing programme through much of Scotland.

Alongside the fight for better housing went the struggle to prevent sharp rises in the rents paid by working class families. Once the industrial warfare of 1919 had subsided, the Government appointed another enquiry to review the case for a return to 'economic' rents at Glasgow and elsewhere. By this time even the owners were concerned at the consequences of a sudden return to the free market, and the panic selling of property which would result.[376] In the event, therefore, the Salisbury Committee recommended limited increases which eventually resulted in a 30% rise in rents plus compensatory charges for rates and improvements since 1914.[377] On hearing of the new rents legislation brought in by the Lloyd George coalition, the Scottish Housing Association mobilised its forces to oppose the implementation. This time the Labour Party took a much more directive role, appointing 'street captains' to marshal the tenants against the factors and administering strike funds on behalf of the residents.[378] Lacking the industrial support of strategic munitions workers, and with a working population already being affected by unemployment, I.L.P. and Labour activists sought desperately to recapture the spirit of the 1915 campaigns. Baillie John Wheatley urged the tenants, that rents were but one element in the defence of working class living standards and the security of the tenements again offered the best chance of success:[379]

They can starve you into acceptance of their terms for food, but the houses are in your own hand, and, if you fight here, you cannot fail!

Rents unrest was apparent not only in Glasgow but in the distinct settlements of Cambuslang, Greenock, Port Glasgow, Paisley and particularly Clydebank, as unemployment climbed steeply from 1921 onwards. That resistance in Clydebank became so marked after 1912 that in early 1925 (following the collapse of the first Labour administration) the Government appointed the Constable Committee of enquiry. As in the 1915 troubles, there was a direct relationship between the dissatisfaction at industrial conditions (more specifically the lack of employment), and the growth of tenant organisation. As Patrick Dollan, a member of the Constable Committee, wrote in his 'minority' view of the unrest, 'The Clyde Rent War!':[380]

The rent struggle in Clydebank, properly understood, is not an antagonism between tenants and owners so much as an expression of discontent by the tenants against an

industrial order which does not afford them a reasonable maintenance.

By this period the Labour Party was already becoming enmeshed in the machinery of local government and had drawn strong criticism from sections of the I.L.P. under Maxton. Much of the ground organisation and street campaigning was left to a rising generation of Communist Party activists at Clydebank and elsewhere. The forms of street politics in London's East End, so vividly described by Phil Piratin, could also be seen at Clydebank in these years.[381]

The contribution which the 1915 rent strikes made to the subsequent organisation of women is more difficult to assess. Working class housewives had undoubtedly provided the backbone of resistance which made the strike campaign possible, and it was their local initiatives which gave such bodies as the Glasgow Women's Housing Association its claim to mass support in the Autumn of 1915. Mary Macarthur, Susan Lawrence and others were successful in sustaining union organisation at the workplace beyond the debacle at Parkhead over female dilutees, though as soon as Gertrude Tuckwell and others had established themselves as effective opponents of the welfare supervisors, the women were facing demobilisation in large numbers. The munition girls and women successfully resisted the pressures drawing them back into the subservience of domestic service, but their industrial base continued to be weaker than men's. In the home, women appear to have established a greater degree of freedom as a result of the rent strikes, as second and even third generations of Barbours participated in local associations and housing struggles as well as explicitly feminist issues.[382] Mary Barbour was herself found testifying to yet another committee on rent restriction following a second World War, in which she joined campaigners such as Dan Rider of the War Rents League.[383]

The political impact of the rent strikes upon the position of women in society was a significant one, as is clear from the upsurge in the numbers of women joining the Labour Party (or I.L.P.) as well as the trade unions during the War.[384] Housewives and female workers were now more prominent in such institutions as the local ward committees and in 1919 Mary Macarthur was elected to the National Executive of the Labour Party itself.[385] The class divisions within the feminist and suffrage movements also began to open up as the War progressed, particularly following the Russian Revolutions of 1917. These developments drove the middle class leadership of the suffrage campaign into a staunchly conservative, pro-War position, with Christabel Pankhurst giving the Clyde industrialists at the end of 1917, an account of what had happened in Russia and coming to speak to them as:[386]

. . . Captains of Industry and to ask that they should preserve discipline in Industrial establishments as unless this was done a state of affairs similar to that existing in Russia at the present time would arise. It had been learned that the Government had surrendered to the strikers at Coventry by agreeing to recognise the Committee of Shop Stewards. She desired the Employers to submit an ultimatum to the Government and request them to abandon the movement to recognise Shop Stewards otherwise serious difficulty would arise in the Clyde District.

Fortunately for the socialist elements of the feminist movement, peace crusaders such as Helen Crawfurd had — largely through their role in the rent strike campaigns — achieved sufficient support to offset this tendency, at least in the Scottish context. It was their ceaseless efforts among working class women, rather than the national leadership of the Pankhursts or the W.S.P.U., which convinced astute politicians like Lloyd George of the need for suffrage concessions in 1918.

CHAPTER ELEVEN

Conclusions: class expression and political organisation

Like so much else in the 'Red Clydeside' era, the Glasgow rent strikes passed into the realm of contemporary legend before the ink was dry on the biographies of its leading lights. In the struggle to assert their claims over this valuable piece of political property, many accounts blurred the finer details of this complex movement and thereby obscured its real significance. Heroic lives of outstanding orators such as James Maxton, attributed to them a place in the rent strikes out of all proportion to the contemporary evidence.[387] Gallacher's portrait of the period at least includes such figures as Mary Barbour and Harry Hopkins, but Shinwell's testament fails to mention the contribution of such activists.[388] More prevalent is the tendency to ascribe a critical part in the developments of 1915 to the individual genius of John Maclean. Important though Maclean unquestionably was in the public denunciation of capitalism and the war, his direct political influence probably never equalled that of Dollan, Crawfurd, Hopkins, McBride, Wheatley and others. Certainly in the rent strikes, the agitation of the B.S.P. came at a later stage in the campaign and *Vanguard* was itself careful to give full credit to leaders such as Andrew McBride.[389]

Subsequent accounts of the rent strikes have tempered much of the uncritical hagiography, whilst reproducing other political emphases which correspond to their understanding of essential working class expression. Thus Hinton's concentrates his analysis upon the issues articulated in the workplace, dismissing the suggestion that serious links between C.W.C. shop stewards such as Kirkwood and Reid and the rents campaigns, and focusing instead upon the dilution struggle as the crucial area of class conflict during the first two years of War on Clydeside. Yet the most serious confrontations of 1915 revolved around the questions of wage increases, Munitions legislation, state coercion of industrial strikers and managerial authority rather than dilution as such. The growing challenge to hierarchical power which was noticeable in both industry and wider society before 1914, culminated in the crisis of authority which marked the transition from a peacetime to a militarised state. Nor was this crisis limited to the productive relations of the industrial workplace, but extended throughout the propertied and legal connections which delineated class boundaries. As one speaker said of the Rent Restriction Bill:[390]

It illustrated very strikingly the disruptive and disintegrating effects of the War. . . . It is a breaking through of the whole of the rules governing private property. It is an invasion of many legal rights hitherto enjoyed.

It was this popular protest at the rule of law which posed such a serious threat to the legitimacy of the state as well as the power of the landlords. Sheriff Lee closed the case against the rent strikers on 17th November, with the acknowledgement of a widespread sense of grievance at high rents and suggested that the tenants were not arguing 'that the law was against them but that they thought there was no law . . . applied to their case at all'.[391] This was only partly correct, for leaders such as Helen Crawfurd left their audiences in no doubt as to the illegality of their actions, but insisted that only 'fair and just' laws could command the respect of a people at war. Only by conceding legislation to meet the case of the rent strikers could the Government be assured of continued support for the legal system as a whole.

The broad question of the rising cost of living continued as a fundamental issue in Wartime politics, with the Commissioners on Industrial Unrest finding in 1917 that the subject 'overshadows and aggravates all the other causes of unrest' — which included the housing problem.[392] Working class families were deeply concerned, as consumers as well as producers, with high prices before and after the introduction of rationing. Attacks on the 'profiteering' practices of industrial and other capitalists also continued, with even the *Athenaeum* accepting the strength of feeling in a situation where high food prices and profiteering 'are closely associated in the public mind'.[393] It was this which the Commissioners on Unrest identified as a widespread interest in economic questions during the War, quite distinct from adherence to revolutionary doctrines.[394] Such a mass concern with the facts of everyday life was undoubtedly assisted by the work of socialists such as Maclean, but it did not originate or develop under their direction. Women living near the cradle of the rent strike in Govan became convinced of the need to resist from their own understanding of hardship and justice, rather than an accurate analysis of interest rates or strategies of exploitation.

This suggests that the relationship between political organisation and working class consciousness is more complex than a Leninist analysis of the 'revolutionary party' acknowledges. Working people succeeded in presenting a fundamental challenge to the propertied interests and the state, despite (and arguably because of) the absence of a revolutionary vanguard of trained cadres. In a perceptive comment on the support offered to the rent strikers, W. C. Anderson emphasised the contribution of socialist agitators, but noted that the rule of the landlords was suddenly challenged by 'hundreds of thousands of discriminating and undiscriminating minds'.[395] There arose a mass resistance to rent rises and landlordism which possessed its own dynamic and significance autonomous from the socialist critique of capitalism, or even the Labour campaign for municipal housing. Socialists won the leadership of this struggle by recognising its limitations as well as its potential, and keeping within the demands which enjoyed general support. It would also be misleading to characterise the rent strikes, as one obituary of Mary Barbour did, as the 'remarkable and spontaneous coming together of active spirits'.[396] The strength and vitality of the rents campaign was only possible because so many organisations and groups within the working class contributed to it. There was no spontaneous expression of class interest, but rather the achievement of class awareness as the result of a series of struggles and alliances which gave an organised form to the feelings of resentment and resistance against the identifiable enemy. Institutions which claimed an independent or apolitical role in working class neighbourhoods (such as the ward committees), joined with the autonomous associations created by the Labour Party in the conduct of the strikes. The experience of strife also threw up a network of local arrangements, such as the 'close committees', which adapted the everyday lifestyles of the tenants to the conditions of warfare.

In the heat of the conflict, there occurred an intensive

period of fresh organisation growth which generated distinct forms of association while transforming many existing institutions into agencies of class expression. There were signs that the array of vigilance committees arising at the workplace were developing links with tenant defence committees, threatening the state with a further integration of industrial and social conflict that promised to politicise the issue of 'profiteering' and authority itself. It was the ability of the I.L.P. and Labour Party to harness this creative upsurge in organisational growth, channeling it in a broad framework of demands and aspirations, that accounts for the remarkable success of strikes. In doing so the Labour leadership was able to translate in a very practical way what the alternative political economy of the working class represented.

SELECTED READING

The following books provide an introduction to the history of Clydeside, though the personal accounts have clearly to be used with some care.

Thomas Bell, *Pioneering Days* Lawrence and Wishart (1941) London.
A. Briggs and J. Saville, (eds.) *Essays in Labour History* (1960 and 1971 volumes) Macmillan London.
R. Challinor, *The Origins of British Bolshevism* Croom Helm (1977) London.
T. Dickson (ed.), *Capital and Class in Scotland* Donald (1982) Edinburgh.
D. Englander, *Landlord and Tenant in Urban Britain 1838-1918* O.U.P. (1983).
W. Gallacher, *Revolt on the Clyde* Lawrence and Wishart (1936) London.
W. M. Haddow, *Socialism in Scotland, its Rise and Progress* Reformers' Bookstall (c. 1920) Glasgow.
J. Hinton, *The First Shop Stewards' Movement* Allen and Unwin (1973) London.
D. Kirkwood, *My Life of Revolt* Harrap (1935) London.
R. McKibbin, *The Evolution of the Labour Party, 1910-1924* O.U.P. (1974).
H. McShane and J. Smith, *No Mean Fighter* Pluto (1978) London.
J. D. Young, *The Rousing of the Scottish Working Class* Croom Helm (1979) London.

REFERENCES

1. Thomas Jones, *Whitehall Diary* Vol. I (1916-1925 [Edited by Keith Middlemass]) Oxford University Press (1969) London; p73, report at entry, 8.2.1919; **2.** *Ibid.*, p74.

3. Eirene White, 'Dr. Thomas Jones: Biographical Note', in *ibid.*, pxxi.

4. *Ibid.*, pxxii. See also the letter to Jones from his mother in South Wales during 1909, referring to the popular aspirations regarding housing.

5. Patrick Geddes, *Cities in Evolution: An introduction to the Town Planning Movement and to the study of Civics* Williams & Northgate (1915) London, p116; **6.** *Ibid.*, p128; **7.** *Ibid.*, p154; **8.** *Ibid.*, pp250-51; **9.** *Ibid.*, p267.

10. M. Swenarton, *Homes Fit for Heroes; The Politics and Architecture of Early State Housing in Britain* Heinemann (1981) London, particularly pp5-47, 67-87, for a good example.

11. F. Engels, *The Condition of the Working Class in England* (1844) Panther (1969 reprint, pp71-72).

12. General Papers of Glasgow City Clerk, 'Reports for the Executive Committee on Housing' Strathclyde Regional Archives. SRA D TC 8/19/7, for some indication of appalling housing conditions.

13. J. Butt, 'Working-Class Housing in Glasgow, 1851-1914' in S. D. Chapman (ed.), *The History of Working Class Housing* David & Charles (1971) Newton Abbot, pp71-74; see also F. Bowmaker, *The Housing of the Working Classes* (1895) London, p17, for similar comments on Newcastle.

14. R. G. Rodger, 'The Invisible Hand' Market Forces, Housing and the Urban Form in Victorian Cities' (1981, forthcoming), pp4-5, 10-11, for a comment.

15. F. Wordsall, *The Tenement: A Way of Life . . . Housing in Glasgow* Chambers (1979) Edinburgh, pp21-25, for comments on the material structure.

16. General Papers of Glasgow City Clerk, 'Housing and the Relaxation of Building Restrictions (12.12.1916)'. Reports from the City Clerk and Surveyor (Lindsay and Drummond) in D TC 8/19/8; Report of City Sanitary Inspector (Peter Fyfe), in *ibid.,* pp7-8.

17. *Glasgow Advertiser and Property Circular* 5.1.1915.

18. House of Commons, *Parliamentary Debates* LXXVI (1915), C1. 454, for Harold Smith of Warrington. 'I have had more practical experience of this class of property than any other Hon. Member...the mortgages of working-men's houses in nine cases out of ten belong to the lower middle class.'

19. *Govan Press* 19.11.1915.

20. D. Englander, 'Landlord and Tenant in Urban Scotland . . .' *S.L.H.S.J.* unpublished), p21; **22.** Ibid.

21. M. Daunton and N. Morgan, 'Factors, Landlords and Tenants: Glasgow, 1890-1914' Economic History Society Conference (1980, unpublished, p21; **22.** *Ibid.*

23. Englander, *loc. cit.,* pp8-9.

24. J. Melling, 'Introduction' t (ed.), *Housing, Social Policy and the State* Croom Helm (1980) London, pp2-36, for some general comments.

25. Lord Hunter and W. R. Scott, *Minutes of Evidence of the Committee appointed to Inquire into the Circumstances Connected with the alleged Rental of Small Dwelling-Houses in Scotland* Cd. 8154 (1916), Evidence of Faulds, Q396-99. (Hereafter referred to as Hunter-Scott Committee, Mins: etc.). William Hunter, Born in 1865 in Ayr, and became an Advocate in 1889. Senator of the College of Justices in Scotland in 1912, and Liberal M.P. for Govan itself, 1910-11 before becoming a life peer. Appointed to the Rents Inquiry in 1915, along with Professor Scott of Glasgow University.

26. J. H. Treble, 'The Market for Unskilled Male Labour in Glasgow. 1891-1914' in I. Macdougall (ed.), *Essays in Scottish Labour History* Robertson (1978) Edinburgh, pp117-18.

27. Rodger, *op. cit.,* pp5-10.

28. C. Richardson, *The Tenements of Partick* Partick Housing Association (1978) Glasgow, *op. cit.,* p93. The figure directly compared with 65 persons for Govan, 60 for Glasgow and only 24 for Paisley; **29.** *Ibid.,* pp91-93, 165; **30.** *Ibid.,* p116; **31.** *Ibid.,* p166; **32.** *Ibid.,* p121; **33.** *Ibid.,* pp107-09.

34. John Nicholson, 'The tale of a tenement' The *Spur* (July 1914), describes a tenement near Glasgow City Chambers as enclosing dwellings which resembled 'a low-roofed twin box — a veritable incubator — with a small aperture at each end for the admission of light.' Nicholson was a painter and socialist campaigner whose efforts parallel those of Robert Tressell at Hastings.

35. Butt, *loc. cit.,* pp59, 80.

36. Professor W. Smart, *The Housing Problem and the Municipality* University of Glasgow Free Lectures (1902), p8, for a contemporary comment.

37. Glasgow City Clerk General Papers, 'Reports for the Executive . . .', D TC 8/19/7, for some cases.

38. Smart, *op. cit.*, pp8-9.

39. J. Butt, 'Working-Class Housing in Glasgow, 1900-39' in I. MacDougall (ed.), *op. cit.*, pp149-52.

40. Butt, *loc. cit.*, p82; Treble, *loc cit.*, p115.

41. Rent Strike oral transcripts: no. 6, Mary Cordiner and H. McShane (1978), for comments on housing conditions and struggles.

42. Butt, loc. cit., (1971), pp78-79.

43. Glasgow City Clerks General Papers, Report of the Sanitary Inspector [Peter Fyfe] . . .' (November 1916) D TC 8/19/8, pp6-8.

44. Presbytery of Glasgow, *Report of the Commission on the Housing of the Poor in relation to their Social Condition* Glasgow Presbytery: Maclehose (1891) Glasgow, pp22-23.

45. Englander, *loc. cit.*, p4: 'There the silent struggle between landlord and tenant was fought with a peculiar savagery.'

46. Supervisory Workers oral transcripts: no. 4, Richard Murdoch (1981), for some comments on Freemasonry amongst supervisors. J. Hamilton Muir, *Glasgow in 1901* Hodge (1901) Edinburgh, p199; H. McShane and J. Smith, *No Mean Fighter* Pluto (1978) London. pp3-23, for some idea of Glasgow during the 1900s and the importance of religious sectarianism.

47. W. H. Fraser, 'Municipal Socialism and Social Policy' S.S.R.C. Conference paper (University of Glasgow, 1978), pp1-6, 10-11, for trades councils in west Scotland; also Fraser, 'Trades Councils in the Labour Movement in Nineteenth Century Scotland' in MacDougall (ed.), *op. cit.*, pp2-24; **48.** *Ibid.*, for argument of relatively greater importance of Scottish trades councils and weakness of trade unionism. The argument for weaker trade unionism and scope for political action and broader coordination of labour is also made in J. Reynolds and K. Laybourn, 'The Emergence of the Independent Labour Party in Bradford' *International Review of Social History* XX (1975), which may help to explain the success of the I.L.P. in both regions.

49. J. Ferguson, *An address to the Citizens of the 25 Wards* [16.8.1902] I.L.P. (1902) Glasgow, p6.

50. *Govan Press* 12.2.1915.

51. Englander, *loc. cit.*, pp9-10.

52. Hunter-Scott Committee, Mins: Q 795-98.

53. *Govan Press* 5.3.1915, for a report of the meeting of the Tenants' Defence Association at Govan; **54.** *Ibid.*

55. C. F. Richardson, *op. cit.*, p131; **56.** *Ibid*; see J. Melling, 'Scottish Industrialists and the changing character of Class Relations in the Clyde Region, 1880-1918' in T. Dickson (ed.), *Capital and Class in Scotland* Donald (1982) Edinburgh, for a discussion of the Partick Civic Guild and its contribution to a 'community' consensus in Partick and similar areas.

57. Rent strike oral transcripts: no. 1, Elizabeth MacNab (1978), for some description in Govan Cross and the social relations which revolved around this intersection in the south Glasgow area.

58. Richardson, *op. cit.*, p32.

59. P. J. Dollan *Jubilee History of the Kinning Park Cooperative Society Ltd.*; K.P.C.S. (1923) Glasgow, p37; **60.** *Ibid.*, p171; **61.** *Ibid.*, p39; **62.** *Ibid.*; **63.** *Ibid.*, p65-68; **64.** *Ibid.*, p94; **65.** *Ibid.*, pp47-38; **66.** *Ibid.*, p65; **67.** *Ibid.*, p174; **68.** *Ibid.*, p48.

69. I.L.P., *Report of the Twentieth Annual Conference of the I.L.P.*

(1912) Broady Collection, Glasgow University Library, ref: A202, p10.

70. Quoted in Richardson, *op. cit.*, p32.

71. I.L.P. *Report on the Fifteenth Annual Conference* (1907) A211, pp20-21; **72.** *Ibid.*, p. 55.

73. I.L.P., *Report of the Seventeenth Annual Conference (1909) A213, p23;* **74.** *Ibid.*, p95.

75. I.L.P., *Report of the Eighteenth Annual Conference* (1910) A214, p75.

76. I.L.P., *Report of the Twenty-first Annual Conference* (1913) A217, p52; **77.** *Ibid.*, pp53-54; **78.** *Ibid.*, p54; **79.** *Ibid.*

80. *The Word* (May 1954); Rent Strike oral transcript: no. 6 Mary Cordiner, for various comments on Helen Crawfurd, and the forthcoming Dictionary of Labour Biography essay on Crawfurd by Helen Corr; for Mary MacArthur see D. E. Martin, 'Mary MacArthur' in J.Bellamy and J. Saville (eds.), *Dictionary of Labour Biography* Vol. II Macmillan (1974) London, pp255-57. W. M. Haddow. *Socialism in Scotland* Reformers' Bookstall (c. 1920) Glasgow, for short biographies of Agnes Dollan and Agnes Hardie; see *Scottish Free* biographies of Agnes Dollan and Agnes hardie; see *Scottish Free Press* (May 1933), for Dollan also.

81. Glasgow Trades Council, Minutes: 13.11.1912, for a deputation which included Jane Allan, Miss Burnett and Mrs Kaye.

82. *Forward* 13.1.1914. Other information was supplied by Dr. Sandra Holton, formerly of the University of Stirling, whose help left me greatly in her debt.

83. I.L.P., *Report of the Nineteenth Annual Conference* (1911) A215, pp101-02.

84. Dollan, *op. cit.*, p175.

85. Grace Kennedy, 'Tribute to a Pioneer' *Govan Press* 8.4.1958, for an obtituary of Mary Barbour from one of her close friends and fellow activists.

86. Rent Strike oral transcript, no. 2, Barbour family and W. McShane (1978), for details of 'Granny' Barbour's life and a family portrait of her; also 'Mary Barbour' in *The Domesday Book of Glasgow,* Strathclyde Regional Archives, SRA LK 1/156.

87. Dollan, *op. cit.*, p93. Dollan suggests that the decision of the Kinning Park Society to maintain rather than raise the rents of its local property in Govan may 'have germinated the famous rent strike which was started by Kinning Park members resident in South Govan'. He goes on to document the origins of the strike: 'These tenants were subjected to an increase of 3/1 per month in rent against which they rebelled. They defied eviction. Their resistance encouraged others to do likewise. The strike against increased rent developed into a national movement, and, before the end of the year, the Government was obliged to pass an Act stabilising house rents at the 1914 level.' Since Dollan was involved in the less celebrated 1920 rent strikes he was concerned to provide a respectable and dramatic genealogy for the rents movements in west Scotland by the time of writing.

88. Andrew McBride, writing in *Forward* 4.12.1915; Letter [from Ben Shaw] in *Forward* 16.1.1915; for conference, See Rent Strike oral transcripts: no. 3, Harry McShane (1978), for some comments on Ben Shaw and Glasgow L.P.

89. *Forward* 9.1.1915.

90. Background information supplied by Sandra Holton from her own research on women's political movements in Scotland.

91. Dollan, *op. cit.,* p46.

92. Rent Strike oral transcripts: no. 6, Mary Cordiner (1978).

93. I.L.P., A202 (1893), p3; **94.** I.L.P., A204 (1895), p14.

95. Dollan, *op. cit.,* p181; D. C. Cummings, *A Historical Survey of the Boilermakers' and Iron and Steel Ship Builders' Society, 1834-1904* Robinson (1905); J. E. Mortimer, *History of Boilermakers' Society* (1973), p149.

96. I.L.P., A216 (1912), pp28-29; **97.** L.C.M.A. Mins: 11.2.1914; **98.** *Ibid.;* **99.** I.L.P., A216 (1912), p97; **100.** I.L.P., A207 (1900), p31; also A208 (1901), p39; **101.** I.L.P., A209 (1902), p31.

102. M. Swenarton, *Homes Fit for Heroes: The Politics and Architecture of Early State Housing in Britain* Heinemann (1981) London, pp5-26 and *passim* for discussion of history and ideology of town planning and design.

103. I.L.P., A212 (1908), p75; **104.** I.L.P., A215 (1911), pp100-01, **105.** I.L.P., A218 (1914), p128; **106.** I.L.P., A215 (1911), pp100, 101-02; **107.** I.L.P., A216 (1912), p103.

108. National Council of British Socialist Sunday Schools, *Socialist Sunday School Song Book* (c. 1932). Copy owned by Mary Thomson of west Scotland in Broady Collection, E3. Song 112, p110, by Felix Adler for example; *c.f.* Song 30, p30, by John Glasse.

109. S. Cooper, 'John Wheatley: A Study in Labour Biography' (Ph.D. Glasgow, 1971), pp15-16.

110. W. H. Fraser, *loc. cit.,* (1978), p11.

111. J. Ferguson, *An Address to the Citizens of the 25 Wards* [16.8.1902] I.L.P. (1902) Glasgow, pp1-5.

112. *Forward* 4.12.1915.

113. Hunter-Scott Committee, Mins: Q 586.

114. *Forward* 7.2.1914, for the support given by John Wheatley to Lord Provost Dunlop on the question of rent books issued to tenants; **115.** *Ibid.* An investigation of some two thousand complaints revealed overcharging to the amount of £478, with almost one quarter of the total complaints arising in the troubled Fairfield ward.

116. *Govan Press* 2.7.1915; McShane and Smith, *op. cit.,* p20, for comments of McShane on the prominence of skilled engineering journeymen in the ranks of the I.L.P.: **117.** *Govan Press* 26.11.1915, for the subsequent part played by Galloway in the rents disturbances.

118. Glasgow Town Clerk Papers, 'Notes prepared for Lord Provost Stevenson, march 30th 1912: subject, Ward Committees' in TC D 6/606/1/43 and also TC D 6/606/12/16. These notes were apparently prepared by John Lindsay.

119. City of Glasgow Municipal Papers, Copy of Gentler's Bill for "Legalizing Ward Committees, 1887" (including ms notes annotated by Gentler) in Strathclyde Regional Archives: SRA MP 16/723; cutting from *Glasgow Herald* 2.12.1887, with report of Fourth Ward Committee meeting in SRA MP 16, p725.

120. Glasgow Corporation Minutes extract in City Chamberlain's Office Papers, 'Notes on G. B. Esskemont (City Chamberlain's Office) dated 16.12.1954', enclosing minute of 18.4.1913. Reference TC D 6/606/12/16. Also minute of 4.6.1914 at *ibid.* These were typescript notes prepared for Judith Hart on the development of local ward committees.

121. 'Notes prepared for Lord Provost Stevenson . . .', *op. cit.,* pp3-4.
122. McShane and Smith, *op. cit.,* for a comment on ward committees.
123. Govan Ward Committee Minutes (First Ward), Minutes 1903-09 in TD 90/2. Minutes: 29.3.1904 — 26.4.1904; **124.** *Ibid.,* Minutes: 5.10.1905, 3.10.1907; see 9.8.1906, for contribution of Galloway; **125.** *Ibid.,* Minutes: 29.9.1909 — 15.9.1910; **126.** *Ibid.,* Minutes: 8.10.1904.
127. Govan Ward Committee Minutes (Central Ward), Minutes: 21.11.1917 — 16.1.1918; **128.** *Ibid.,* Minutes: 16.10.1918 — 18.10.1918.
129. Maryhill Ward Committee Minutes (Eighteenth Ward), Attendance Roll of the Maryhill Committee (1920-49) in SRA TD 455/6, for individuals.
130. J. Hinton, *The First Shop Stewards' Movement* Allen & Unwin (1973) London, p122. R. Challinor, *The Origins of British Bolshevism* Croom Helm (1977) London.
131. B. Holton, *British Syndicalism, 1900-14* Pluto (1976) London pp40-41. W. Kendall, *The Revolutionary Movement in Britain, 1900-21* Weidenfeld & Nicolson (1969) London, p60.
132. Kendall, *ibid.,* p63. Neil Maclean went on to found the Partick branch of the I.L.P. and to serve as Labour M.P. for Govan and was subsequently accused of financial malpractice, being disowned by his local party branch.
133. Hinton, *op. cit.,* p122; **134.** *Ibid.*
135. *Forward* 6.8.1910 for contribution of Maclean in Nan Milton (ed.), *John Maclean: In the Rapids of Revolution* Alison & Busby (1978); see also P. Adelman, *The Rise of the Labour Party, 1880-1945* Longmans (1972), p43.
136. *Forward* 13.8.1910 in Milton, *op. cit.,* Adelman, *op. cit.,* p44.
137. *Pollockshaws News* 23.3.1904 — 8.4.1904, in Milton, *op. cit.*
138. W. Gallacher, *Revolt on the Clyde* (1936) Lawrence & Wishart reprint (1978), p54-57.
139. Hinton, *op. cit.,* p118; J. McHugh, 'The Clyde Rent Strike' *Journal Scottish Labour History Society* XI (1978), for very similar interpretation.
140. W. R. Scott and R. Cunnison, *The Industries of the Clyde Valley during the War* Oxford University Press (1924), pp74-75, 114-17; Hinton, *op. cit.,* p109. Professor Scott had sat with Lord Hunter in the rents enquiry and was only one in the crowd of distinguished economists, historians and jurists who intervened in Scottish public life from the late 19th century onwards, following (as he did) the precepts of Adam Smith in his understanding of economic change and political expediency during the War.
141. North West Engineering Trades Employers' Association, Minutes: 15.6.1914.
142. H. Wolfe, *Labour Supply and Regulation* C.U.P. (1923). P116.
143. N.W.E.T.E.A. Minutes: 24.8.1914; **144.** N.W.E.T.E.A. Minutes: 15.1.1915; **145.** *Ibid.,* Gallacher refers to Bunton as 'Binton'; **146.** N.W.E.T.E.A. Minutes: 19.1.1915; **147.** N.W.E.T.E.A. Minutes: 25.1.1915 — 19.1.1915; **148.** N.W.E.T.E.A. Minutes: 10.2.1915, for offer to Steam Engine Makers and United Machine Workers' Association; **149.** N.W.E.T.E.A. Minutes: 17.2.1915; **150.** N.W.E.T.E.A minutes: 18.2.1915; **151.** N.W.E.T.E.A. Minutes: 18.2.1915; **152.** N.W.E.T.E.A. Minutes: 20.2.1915.
153. Hinton, *op. cit.,* pp106-07.
154. N.W.E.T.E.A., Minutes: 22.2.1915; **155.** N.W.E.T.E.A. Minutes;

20.2.1915; **156.** *Ibid.*; **157.** N.W.E.T.E.A. Minutes: 2.3.1915; Hinton, *op. cit.*, pp106-08; **158.** N.W.E.T.E.A. Minutes: 2.3.1915; **159.** N.W.E.T.E.A. Minutes: 23.3.1915, 27.3.1915, 30.3.1915; **160.** N.W.E.T.E.A. Minutes: 18.6.1915.

161. The existence of the Armaments Committee remains shadowy, and it appears to have been ineffective in the face of continuing difficulties and disagreements over industrial production during 1915.

162. *Parliamentary Debates, op. cit.*, LXXII (23.6.1915), C1. 1129.30 for comments of Pringle.

163. Gallacher, *op. cit.*, p63; Hinton, *op. cit.*, p113.

164. *History of the Ministry of Munitions* H.M.S.O. (1922) IV pt.ii. pp50-54; **165.** *Ibid., Forward* 4.9.1915.

166. *H.M.M., op. cit.*; **167.** *Ibid.*, p56; Hinton, *op. cit.*, pp116-17.

168. C. Addison, *Four and Half Years* 2 Vols (1934), Entry 12.10.1915.

169. The Commission was to resume sitting in early November, reporting to the Government at the end of the year.

170. Sharp reported in *Govan Press* 22.10.1915.

171. *H.M.M., op. cit.*, pp59-60.

172. Hinton, *op. cit.*, p118.

173. *H.M.M.*, IV pt.iv pp98-99.

174. N.W.E.T.E.A. Minutes: 18.9.1915; **175.** Letter at N.W.E.T.E.A. Minutes: 25.10.1915; **176.** N.W.E.T.E.A. Minutes: 6.12.1915; B. Drake, *Women in the Engineering Trades* (1971) London, p27; **177.** N.W.E.T.E.A. Minutes: 6.12.1915.

178. Hunter-Scott Committee, *Minutes . . .* Q70, for Walker Smith's figures.

179. Report of Glasgow Town Clerk and City Surveyor 'The proposed relaxation of building restriction . . .' (12.12.1916) DTC 8/19/8.

180. F. E. Freemantle, *The Housing of the Nation* Allan (1925), pp22-23.

181. *Glasgow Advertiser and Property Circular* 5.1.1915; *Govan Press* 19.11.1915, for appraisals of Wartime changes.

182. Addison, *op. cit.*, Entry 29.9.1915.

184. *Forward* 29.8.1914; McShane and Smith, *op. cit.*, pp24-25, describing Tom Kerr as one of the 'outstanding agitators' of 1908 unemployment protests; **185.** *Ibid.*; **186.** *Forward* 21.11.1914; **187.** *Forward* 26.12.1914.

188. Glasgow Trades Council, Minutes: 17.12.1914.

189. *Forward* 23.1.1915.

190. Glasgow Trades Council, Minutes: 17.2.1915; **191.** Glasgow Trades Council, Minutes: 21.4.1915; Patrick Geddes noted in his major work of 1915, that the arrival of Woolwich workers to the Clyde district had provoked various difficulties, including reluctance of the London immigrants to accept tenement accommodation near the torpedo works (Presumably the Greenock site) and that the 'needful discontent' resulted in a healthy creation of cottage accommodation. Geddes, *op. cit.*, p141. **192.** Glasgow Trades Council, Minutes: 5.5.1915; **193.** Glasgow Trades Council, Minutes: 20.1.1915.

194. Handbill of Glasgow Women's Housing Association, Library of Patrick Dollan, entitled: 'Meeting of Women' for 16.2.1915 at 3 pm. Handbill in possession of L. Rosenberg, Glasgow.

195. *Forward* 29.5.1915, for Letter of Patrick Dollan.

196. *Govan Press* 12.2.1915. There was often some substance to the claim that patriotic servicemen and pensioners were threatened by the general pressure upon accommodation and rents, as the records of the Partick Civic Guild demonstrate. In Spring 1915, the Prince of Wales Fund referred the case of James Miller to the Guild, described as 'a pensioner who served in the Afghan War, and who now resides at 37 Orchard Street, Partick. He is about 68 years of age and a French polisher to trade and was unemployed owing to the War. Recently he got employment, but owing to old age, he was unable to fulfil his duties, with the result that he is now unemployed'. Partick Civic Guild, Minutes: 4.5.1915. There was also the case of a Whiteinch family reported earlier in the year, with the father having fallen much behind with his rent. Although the man was able to find work and feed his ill wife and children, the factor had taken steps to have him evicted. See *ibid.,* Minutes: 17.2.1915; **197.** *Govan Press* 12.2.1915, commented that the general rise in prices and shortage of housing gave 'the factors and "lairds" a monopoly by means of which they can demand any rent they please . . .'; *History of Ministry . . .,* IV pt.ii, pp37-38; **198.** *Forward* 5.6.1915; **199.** *Govan Press* 28.5.1915. The women were Mrs Clark, Hill, Spiers and Thom; **200.** *Forward* 5.6.1915. It is not clear whether these two meetings were the same or similar events; **201.** Forward 5.6.1915-12.6.1915.

202. Oral Transcript No. 1 (14.8.1978) Elizabeth and Mary McNab; Oral Transcript No. 2, *op. cit.,* Barbour family.

203. *Govan Press* 4.6.1915; *Forward* 5.6.1915-12.6.1915; **204.** *Govan Press* 4.6.1915; **205.** *Forward* 5.6.1915 printed them after other newspapers had done so.

206. Glasgow Corporation, Minutes: 14.10.1915, p2484; *Govan Press* 18.6.1915; *Forward* 19.6.1915.

207. *Forward* 10.7.1915.

208. John Broom, *John Maclean* Macdonald (1973) Loanhead, p56.

209. *Glasgow Herald* 7.6.1915; **201.** *Forward* 19.6.1915; Cooper, *op. cit.,* pp80-81; **211.** *Forward* 12.6.1915; **212.** *Glasgow Advertiser and Property Circular* 5.1.1915; **213.** *Forward* 26.6.1915; **214.** *Ibid.;* **215.** *Forward* 19.6.1915; **216.** *Glasgow Advertiser and Property Circular* 4.5.1915; *c.f. Glasgow Advertiser . . .* 30.3.1915, for a vehement attack on the 'traitorous voice of the "Ca'cannyist" . . .'; **217.** *Govan Press 2.7.1915;* **218.** *Govan Press* 9.7.1915.

219. *Parliamentary Debates, op. cit.,* LXXII (23.6.1915), Cl.1601, for contribution of Pringle.

220. Sir. C. Petrie, *Walter Long and His Times* (1937), pp188-97.

221. *Forward* 28.8.1915; **222.** *Ibid.*; **223.** *Ibid.*; **224.** *Govan Press* 27.8.1915; *Glasgow Herald* 27.8.1915; **225.** *Govan Press* 3.9.1915; **226.** *Govan Press* 10.9.1915; **227.** *Govan Press* 24.9.1915; **228.** *Glasgow Herald* 9.9.1915; **229.** *Bulletin* 29.9.1915; **230.** *Govan Press* 10.9.1915; **231.** *Bulletin* 29.9.1915; **232.** *Partick and Maryhill Press* 1.10.1915.

233. Oral Transcript No. 5 (17.8.1978), *op. cit.,* Jimmy Macfarlane.

234. *Glasgow Herald* 29.9.1915; **235.** *Bulletin* 8.10.1915; **236.** *Glasgow Herald* 23.10.1915; **237.** *Forward* 2.10.1915; **238.** *Bulletin* 29.9.1915, in a report which credits local menfolk with the initiative in beginning the rent strikes.

239. Haddow, *op. cit.,* for some details on Helen Crawfurd. Another clergyman involved at this time was Rev. J. Campbell.

240. *Govan Press* 17.9.1915.

241. Glasgow Corporation, Minutes: 23.9.1915, p2392.

242. *Govan Press* 1.10.1915.

243. Hinton, *op. cit.,* p115.

244. Letter reprinted in *Forward* 9.10.1915. Kirkwood's subsequent account in his autobiography, published twenty years after these events, stressed the connections between the various industrial, rents and political agitations, though his sense of chronology is more hazy (if also less dramatised) than Gallacher's. Kirkwood suggested that the evictions of servicemen's dependents began the protest movement, and says of his own role, that:

I found myself up to the ears in an organized campaign for resistance to the increased rents. John Wheatley, James Stewart, and Rosslyn Mitchell, all of whom subsequently sat with me in the House of Commons, carried out a platform campaign for the building of houses with money provided by the Common Good of the City and grants from the Government, free of interest.

This version suggests how deeply the M.P.'s vision had been coloured by his life on the parliamentary benches, with hardly any credit given to the activists who dominated the street politics of the War. Kirkwood, *My Life of Revolt* Harrap (1935) London, pp119-21. The Parkhead convener's peculiar intimacy with William Beardmore at the Forge again dominates the Labour leader's reminiscences.

245. *Govan Press* 8.10.1915; *Glasgow Herald* 8.10.1915; **246.** *Glasgow Herald* 8.10.1915 for photographs of marchers; *Bulletin* 13.10.1915-18.10.1915; **247.** *Forward* 16.10.1915; **248.** *Govan Press* 15.10.1915; *Glasgow Herald* 13.10.1915; **249.** *Glasgow Herald* 13.10.1915; **250.** *Vanguard* December 1915; **251.** *Glasgow Advertiser and Property Circular* 12.10.1915; *Glasgow Herald* 12.10.1915; **252.** *Govan Press* 15.10.1915; *History of Ministry . . ., op. cit.,* p58;**253.** *Ibid.*; **254.** *Glasgow Herald* 15.10.1915; **255.** *Ibid.*; **256.** *Glasgow Herald* 19.19.1915; **257.** *Glasgow Advertiser and Property Circular* 26.10.1915.

258. Professor W. R. Scott Collection, UG MS GEN 511: Letter to C. R. Fay, 3.12.1939; and others.

259. *Glasgow Herald* 18.10.1915; **260.** *Ibid.*

261. *Glasgow Herald* 20.19.1915-22.10.1915. This report refers to a prosecution at the Summary Eviction Court rather than the Sma-- Debts Court. A man from Hutton Drive, Govan, also charged; **262.** *Govan Press* 19.11.1915; **263.** *Glasgow Herald* 22.10.1915; **264.** *Govan Press* 18.6.1915; **265.** *Glasgow Herald* 22.10.1915; **266.** *Forward* 23.10.1915, for article of Patrick Dollan; **267.** *Glasgow Herald* 23.10. 1915; Oral Transcript No. 2 *op. cit.,* Barbour family; Shinwell letter to present author (1978); suggest that this woman may have been Mrs Noble of Govan.

268. Hunter-Scott Committee, *Minutes . . .,* Q586-89, for evidence of Andrew McBride.

269. *Glasgow Herald* 17.11.1915, gives summary of figures to be found in Appendices of *Report* of Committee of Enquiry.

270. Hunter-Scott Committee, *Minutes . . .,* Q897-99, for David Wardley's evidence; **271.** *Ibid.,* Q991-95, for evidence of Andrew Hood.

272. *History of Ministry . . .,* IV pt iv, p48.

273. *The Times* 8.10.1915-9.10.1915, for reports of rent strikes at Partick and Springburn.

274. P. Watchman, 'The Origin of the 1915 Rent Act' *Law & State* No. 5 (1980), pp31-32, for a quote of Shipwrights' resolution.

275. *History of the Ministry . . .,* IV pt ii, pp59-60; Hinton, *op. cit.,* p118; **276.** *Ibid.,* p119.

277. *Glasgow Herald* 21.10.1915, 26.10.1915, for reports of Kinning Park and Whiteinch respectively; **278.** *Glasgow Herald* 27.10.1915; **279.** *Glasgow Herald* 26.10.1915-27.10.1915.

280. Glasgow Trades Council, Minutes: 20.10.1915-27.10.1915.

281. *Glasgow Herald* 26.10.1915; **282.** *Glasgow Herald* 21.10.1915; **283.** *Glasgow Herald* 22.10.1915; **284.** *Glasgow Herald* 23.10.1915, 1.11.1915, for Coyle and Ferguson respectively; **285.** *Glasgow Advertiser and Property Circular* 19.10.1915; *Bulletin* 8.10.1915.

286. Hunter-Scott Committee, *Minutes* . . ., Q998-99 Q1013-14, Andrew Hood.

287. *Partick and Maryhill Press* 1.10.1915.

288. Hunter-Scott Committee, *Minutes* . . ., Q592; **289.** *Ibid.,* Q991-95, Andrew Hood; **290.** *Ibid.,* Q995; **291.** *Ibid.,* Q998-99, 1013-14.

292. *The Baillie* 20.10.1915, for the amused comment of this popular magazine on the Battle of Thornwood Avenue and its part in the 'Great Social War'.

293. *Forward* 23.10.1915; **294.** *Forward* 30.10.1915.

295. *History of the Ministry* . . ., IV pt.ii, pp59-61.

296. Glasgow Trades Council, Minutes: 9.6.1915, 6.10.1915, 3.11.1915.

297. R. Harrison, 'The War Emergency Workers' National Committee, 1914-1920' in A. Briggs and J. Saville (eds.), *Essays in Labour History 1886-1923* Macmillan (1971), p233, for Letter of Ben Shaw to Middleton on 10.11.1915; **298.** *Ibid.,* pp 233-34.

299. Glasgow Trades Council, Minutes: 3.11.1915.

300. H. McShane, *John Maclean* (September 1940) CP Pamphlet, pp7-11.

301. *Forward* 13.11.1915.

302. Linthouse Papers, *Linthouse Magazine* I No. 3 (March 1920), shows that of £14,450 collected for War Relief Fund in this shipyard firm, almost came from employees and £5,753 (40% of total expenditure) went on rent relief for local working people.

303. Gallacher, *op. cit.,* pp53-54, for this Small Debt Court strategy.

304. *Partick and Maryhill Press* 19.5.1915; *Glasgow Herald* 15.11.1915.

305. *Glasgow Herald* 18.11.1915.

306. McShane and Smith, *op. cit.,* p76 for note on James Reid.

307. *History of the Ministry* . . ., IV pt.ii, Appendix III, p105 reports that Barclay Curles, Coventry Ordnance, Fairfields, Harland and Wolff, Hendersons and Stephens all stopped work in support of the strike. These works were concentrated in the Govan and Partick-Whiteinch-Scotstoun area, and noticeably did not include Beardmores of Dalmuir or John Browns of Clydebank.

308. Broom, *op. cit.,* p65.

309. *Forward* 27.11.1915. There were a number of distinct accounts of these events but Gallacher's is probably suspect; **310.** *Ibid.*; **311.** *Glasgow Herald* 18.11.1915, largely reproduced in *Forward* 27.11.1915; **312.** *Forward* 27.11.1915; **313.** *Glasgow Herald* 18.11.1915.

314. *History of Ministry . . ., op. cit.*

315. *The Times* 19.11.1915, 2.12.1915.

316. D. E. Martin, 'W. C. Anderson (1877-1919)', *Dictionary of Labour Biography,* II, *op. cit.,* pp12.13.

317. *Forward* 13.11.1915, for W. C. Anderson's appraisal.

318. *Parliamentary Debates, op. cit.,* CI 758-59 for Hugh Law's comment on Long's introduction of legislation and the munitions production districts.

319. *Glasgow Advertiser and Property Circular* 30.11.1915; **320.** *Glasgow Herald* 18.10.1915, 28.10.1915, **321.** *The Times* 8.10.1915-9.10.1915,

11.10.1915, 30.10.1915; and also Harry McShane, 'The Rents Struggle' in *Forward* 24.10.1953, for a heroic and valuable presentation of the campaigns; **322.** *Glasgow Herald* 15.10.1915, 20.10.1915, 17.11.1915; **323.** *Forward* 30.10.1915.

324. R. B. Stucke (ed.), *Fifty Years History of the Woolwich Labour Party, 1903-53* Woolwich Labour Party (1953), pp7-12, 77 and *passim*; **325.** *Ibid.,* p17; also G. Crossick, *An Artisan Elite in Victorian Society* Croom Helm (1978) London, pp243-47, for some comments on the *Woolwich Pioneer.*

326. Stucke, *op. cit.,*p24; P. Thompson, *Socialists, Liberals and Labour: the struggle for London, 1885-1914* Routledge & Kegan Paul (1967) London, pp256-64; **327.** Stucke, *op. cit.,* pp19-21.

328. D. Hopkin, 'The Membership of the I.L.P., 1904-1910 . . .' *International Review of Social History* XX (1975), pp185-87, 193 and *passim*; **329.** *Ibid.,* pp193-95.

330. *Woolwich Pioneer* 28.5.1915-4.6.1915, where reports of rents discontent are reported in the columns of "Free Lance" (William Barefoot), alongside extended reports of wages unrest and demands for improved conditions amongst the Arsenal foremen and supervisory grades; **331.** *Woolwich Pioneer* 30.4.1915; **332.** *Woolwich Pioneer* 28.5.1915; **333.** Letter from Ada Jennings in *Woolwich Pioneer* 4.6.1915; **334.** *Woolwich Pioneer* 28.5.1915-4.6.1915; also Deborah Thom, "Women Munitions Workers at Woolwich Arsenal in the 1914-18 War" M.A. Thesis (Warwick, 1975), pp106-08 and *passim* for useful background details. I am grateful to Deborah for permission to cite her original study.

335. Swenarton, *op. cit.,* pp53-58, for a discussion. **336.** Quoted in *The Times* 15.10.1915; **337.** *Glasgow Herald* 25.11.1915; **338.** *Glasgow Herald* 19.11.1915.

339. Original handbill from the Patrick Dollan library, headed "Great Public Procession and Demonstration" in the possession of Lou Rosenberg, Glasgow.

340. *Glasgow Herald* 25.11.1915, for the meeting and another addressed by McBride at Pollockshaws (John Maclean's original campaigning area) the same evening.

341. *Parliamentary Debates, op. cit.,* Cl. 422 for Walter Long; **342.** *Ibid.,* Cl. 1519, for Long at the Second Reading of the Bill; **343.** *Ibid.,* Cl. 461-62 for Mackinder; **344.** *Ibid.,* Cl 726-27 for Tudor Walter.

345. *The Times* 28.10.1915, has a report of the views of Lord Desborough of the Land Union; **346.** *Glasgow Advertiser and Property Circular* 19.10.1915, for an adverse reference to the Irish Rent Court. These comments should be set in the context of the highly-charged political and military situation in Ireland during the early years of the War, particularly Easter 1916. See fn. 366 below.

347. *Parliamentary Debates, op. cit.,* Cl. 463, for Mackinder; **348.** *Ibid.,* C1. 1687-88, for George Barnes on the Bill.

349. A. M'Neil, *The Increase of Rent and Mortgate Interest... Acts* Hodge (1919) Glasgow, pp3-5 and *passim.*

350. *The Times* 26.11.1915.

351. *Parliamentary Debates, op. cit.,* C1. 733 for the remarks made by Whittacker; **352.** *Ibid.,* C1. 749 for Barnes; **353.** *Ibid.,* C1. 2313 for Long's response.

354. *Govan Press* 3.12.1915.

355. *Parliamentary Debates, op. cit.,* C1. 1515-17, 1472-73, for Barnes and Millar respectively.

356. *Govan Press* 3.12.1915.

357. Englander, *loc. cit.*, for an outline of subsequent ejectment patterns.

358. A. Clinton, 'Trades Councils During the First World War' *International Review of Social History* XV (1970), p211.

359. Harrison, *loc. cit.*, p242.

360. Clinton, *loc. cit.*, p209, pp214-15.

361. *The Times* 2.11.1915, for a report of the "Workers' War Emergency Committee" and its activities in organising conferences for local Tenants' Defence leagues; **362.** *The Linthouse Magazine*, Stephens company has some of the details; **363.** *Govan Press* 19.11.1915.

364. McShane, *op. cit.* (1941), for a sympathetic account of Maclean's career.

365. *Vanguard* December 1915.

366. Hinton, *op. cit.*, pp128-35. It is significant that Kirkwood refers to the Irish situation and the implications for the Scottish popular politics in his account of the crisis of early 1916. Commenting on the arrest and subsequent imprisonment of John Muir for offences connected with *The Worker* (as distinct from *Vanguard*), Kirkwood suggested that much deeper concern amongst the government was provoked by the discovery in the newspaper offices of some 'copies of an Irish paper containing a foolish and flaming article by the Countess Markowizt. Great play was made of those papers.' Kirkwood, *op. cit.*, pp118-19. Although most accounts of the War and its labour troubles make little reference to the gathering Irish storm, the outbreak of the Irish rebellion of Easter 1916, with its divisive consequences for political and religious forces in west Scotland, must have contributed to the disarray of the Labour movement at Glasgow and elsewhere at that time.

367. Clyde Shipbuilders' Association, Minutes: 21.3.1916.

368. United Boilermakers' Society, *Monthly Report* (March 1916), p71, for the speech of David Redpath (who had been a champion of the rivetters' claims in the 1902 Municipal Commission on Housing). I owe this reference to Alastair Reid. The implied gulf of experience between male workers and women concerned with domestic issues and particularist organisations was not wholly justified. In 1902 the Boilermakers' Society in west Scotland had taken part in a large demonstration, reputedly involving fifty trade unions and 30,000 trade unionists at Glasgow, to 'protest against the Taff Vale judgement and to call for better housing for Glasgow workers.' See. J. Mortimer, *History of the Boilermakers' Society, 1834-1906* Allen & Unwin (1973) London, p147. The Govan contingent of the Society displayed tools loaned by their brethren in Clydebank for the day.

369. Glasgow Independent Labour Party, Minutes at Mitchell Library, Glasgow. ML G 329.9, Executive Committee Minutes (1917-19), Minute: 7.9.1917.

370. *Forward* Claimed that 15,000 Glasgow households were on rent strike by late-October 1915, with Patrick Dollan suggesting that this later rose to 25,000 people actively supporting the anti-landlord cause.

371. Hunter-Scott Committee, *Minutes*, Q 69, for evidence for Walker Smith.

372. *Parliamentary Debates, op. cit.*, C1. 787-88, for comment of Essex that 'those who have seen it in operation, and those who will have benefited from its operation — make no doubt about it! — will never forget the lesson.'

373. McLean, *op. cit.,* pp267-68, for the subsequent progress of the Scottish Housing Association.

374. Ministry of Reconstruction, *Report on the Increase of Rent and Mortgage Interest Acts* Cd. 9235 (1919), p5 paras. 12-15.

375. Butt, *loc, cit.* (1978), pp150-54.

376. Ministry of Health (Departmental Committee), *Report on the Increase of Rent and Mortgage Interests Acts* Cmd. 658 (1920). p1, para. 4.

377. John Wheatley, *The New Rent Act: A Reply to the Rent Raisers* Scottish Labour Housing Association (1920, Glasgow p8).

378. McLean, *op. cit.,* pp267-68.

379. Wheatley, *op. cit.,* pp8-9.

380. P. Dollan, *The Clyde Rent War!* Independent Labour Party/Civic Press (1925), p8.

381. P. Piratin, *Our Flag Stays Red* Lawrence & Wishart (1948, reprint 1980), London, pp37-45 and *passim.*

382. Oral history transcript, No. 2 for accounts of the Barbour family.

383. Ministry of Health (Scotland), *Report of the Inter-Departmental Committee on Rent Control* Cmd. 6621 (1945), para. 17 and Appendices, which gives Mary Barbour as one of the witnesses. This Committee reported to ex-editor of *Forward* and now Secretary of State for Scotland, Thomas Johnston.

384. A. J. B. Marwick, 'The Independent Labour Party in the Nineteen Twenties' *Bulletin of Institute of Historical Research* XXXV (1962), pp66-68 and *passim* for subsequent developments.

385. D. E. Martin, 'Mary Macarthur', *loc. cit.,* p258.

386. N.W.E.T.E.A. Minutes: 16.12.1917, for the visit of Mrs Pankhurst.

387. E. Shinwell, *Conflict Without Malice* Odhams (1955) London, p63, for a photograph of Hopkins without any comment in the text. Harry McShane suggests that Hopkins subsequently descended to alcoholism and an unrespectable domestic lifestyle of squalor and poverty.

388. John McNair, *James Maxton: The Beloved Rebel* (1955), p52, for example.

389. *Vanguard December 1915, referred to the 'tireless energy of Mr McBride; in a curious return* compliment, *Forward* during the Second World War suggested that John MacLean had personally 'led strikes against the exorbitant rents charged in overcrowded Glasgow'. See *Forward* 27.11.1943. This says as much about the changing perspectives on the interwar years and attitudes to Labour luminaries, as about the making of the Maclean legend and the hagiography constructed around this 'martyr of class struggle', as McShane and others remember him.

390. *Parliamentary Debates, op. cit.,* C1. 787-88.

391. Sheriff Lee as quoted in the *Glasgow Herald* 18.11.1915.

392. Commission of Enquiry into Industrial Unrest, *Reports of the Commissioners for Scotland* Cd. 8669 (1917), p4, para. 8.

393. *Anon., 'Labour Unrest: An Unofficial Inquiry', Athenaeum* (Supplement) July 1917, pp i-11.

394. Commission of Enquiry into Industrial Unrest, *op. cit.*

395. *Forward* 13.11.1915.

396. Baillie Jack Davies, 'The End of an Epoch' *Govan Press* (April 1958), an obituary cutting in the possession of the Barbour family.